ADVANCE PRAISE

"A moving account of a son in search of his father and the home from which his family was expelled. Peter Kupfer's compelling story leads deep into the abyss of a small Bavarian town during Nazi Germany and into the labyrinth of the human soul. Anyone who is interested in exploring their family roots and in reconciliation with a difficult past should read this book."

– Michael Brenner, Director of the Center for Israel Studies at American University and International President of the Leo Baeck Institute for the Study of German-Jewish History.

"This is a wonderful piece of work ... compelling throughout; elegantly weaves the chilling history of German antisemitism with personal family history. ... The descriptions of family life in Connecticut wield significant emotional power. It feels like you're taken back in time and are the fly on the wall during critical family interactions."

– Matthew Isaac Sobin, author of *The Last Machine in the Solar System*

THE GLASSMAKER'S SON

LOOKING FOR THE WORLD MY FATHER LEFT BEHIND IN NAZI GERMANY

PETER KUPFER

ISBN 9789493276642 (ebook)

ISBN 9789493276468 (paperback)

ISBN 9789493276499 (hardcover)

Publisher: Amsterdam Publishers, The Netherlands

info@amsterdampublishers.com

The Glassmaker's Son is part of the Series **Holocaust Survivor True Stories WWII**

Copyright © Peter Kupfer 2022

Cover image: Dad and granddad on San Marco square in Venice, circa 1935

All Rights Reserved. No part of this publication may be reproduced or transmitted in any form or by any means, electronic or mechanical, including photocopy, recording or any other information storage and retrieval system, without prior permission in writing from the publisher.

CONTENTS

Prologue	1

PART I

The World Left Behind	7
Weiden in der Oberpfalz	10
'The Lords Are Coming'	22
Confusion at the Cemetery	34

PART II

Starting Over	49
Getting Out	55
Stormy Wedding	60
Matriarchy	66
Willow Street	72
Big Gert and Little Bob	75
Different Dad	79
Matinee	86
Showroom	90
Drugs, Deadheads, and Divine Light	95
Gay Boy	98

PART III

Lost Portraits	105
The Quest	113
Glass Dynasty	119
A Brief History of Antisemitism in Germany	128
Gathering Storm	131
Daily Torment	135
Kristallnacht and Beyond	141
Otto's Choice	150
A Retirement Home in Bohemia	153

PART IV

Dad's Silence	167
On the Fence	170

Getting Closer — 173
Final Days — 179
The Good China — 187

PART V
Guest of the City — 193
Eduard and Fanni Return — 199
Terezín Tourist — 206
Back to Weiden — 214
Article 116 — 220

Afterword — 223
Acknowledgments — 225
Selected Bibliography — 229
Notes — 231
Amsterdam Publishers Holocaust Library — 243

For my father

PROLOGUE

On the morning of my 35th birthday, July 18, 1986, I walked into probate court in New Haven to change my name. I was born a Cooper, the name my father adopted after he immigrated to the United States from Germany in 1937. Dad's original name was Kupfer, but like many other Jewish immigrants he anglicized it in an effort to blend into his new country and distance himself from his past. Now, 10 years after his death, I was going to change it back.

On top of all the other losses my father had suffered as a result of the Holocaust, it had robbed him of his identity. I couldn't make up for those other losses, but at least I could save the family name. By reclaiming it I was making a statement to the world: I am proud of my father, proud of my heritage, and I'm not going to let the Nazis or anyone else deprive me of my true identity. Besides, I never much cared for the name Cooper. It was so common and Waspy sounding.

My mother was puzzled by my decision. How would people find me? What about all my official documents – driver's license, passport, Social Security card? Cooper is the name you were born with, the name of your mother and brother. Why do you always have to be different?

In the hushed, half-empty courtroom, I waited nervously as the judge disposed of one case after another, mostly disputes over wills, with peevish dispatch. When the clerk called my name, I stood up, the judge asked me a few questions, slapped his gavel on the bench, and voila! Peter Cooper was no more. I was now Peter Kupfer.

I walked out of the courthouse feeling proud of myself and imagined that my father would have been proud of me too, but there were no toasts or celebratory dinners. Other than my mother and brother, I didn't tell anyone what I had done, not even my boss at the *Bridgeport Post*, where I worked as a reporter. It wasn't until five years later, when I moved to California to take a job as a copyeditor at the *San Francisco Chronicle*, that I began to use my new name. I was starting a new job in a new city where I didn't know a soul and not a soul knew me, so the time was right.

I had hoped to pass my father's name on to children of my own one day, but as a gay man who grew up in an era when same-sex parents were rare and same-sex marriage almost unimaginable, being a parent wasn't in the cards. So it appears my father's name will die with me, but I'm still glad I went to probate court that day.

When I think about my father, the image that comes to mind is always a little hazy. I was 25 when he died and we lived under the same roof for the better part of 20 years, yet in some ways he was always a mystery to me. He was a good man, a kind man, that much I knew, but his innermost thoughts and deepest feelings were mostly hidden from view. I never saw him cry, rarely heard him raise his voice in anger or excitement. I never had any doubt that he loved me, as I loved him, but I don't recall him ever uttering the words, "I love you."

Dad was by nature quiet and reflective, but circumstances no doubt contributed to his reticence. He was 30 years old when he fled Nazi Germany and, like other refugees before and since, he left behind family, friends, language, and culture to start a new life in a country where he knew virtually no one. His father and many other members of his family were murdered in concentration camps. Given that harrowing history, it's hardly surprising that he, like so many other Holocaust survivors, preferred to stay low to the ground, to blend in and get along rather than draw attention to himself.

And then there was my mother and her family. The daughter of Ukrainian Jewish immigrants, Mom was a strong-willed, demanding woman who evinced more than enough emotion for two. She was the undisputed commander-in-chief of the family, the setter and enforcer of domestic policy, czarina of household operations, and director-general of social activities. And that was just fine with Dad.

From time to time my father spoke about going back to Germany. He and my mother went to Europe several times to see the sights and visit relatives in France and England, but something always came up that prevented them from returning to his homeland. The real reason, I suspect, was that his heart wasn't in it. The prospect of stirring up the ghosts of his former life was too painful to bear.

This book is, first of all, an effort to piece together the missing puzzle parts of my father's life. Who was this soft-spoken, inscrutable man with a guttural accent and a mischievous sense of humor? A man I loved dearly yet knew so little about.

It's also an effort to figure out who I am. For better or worse, I inherited many of my father's traits, including his tendency to observe the world from a distance rather than engage with it directly and to keep other people at arm's length. Through the process of writing this book I have come to understand that my father's absence, as much as his presence, has had a profound effect on my life.

PART I

THE WORLD LEFT BEHIND

My father rarely spoke about his life in Germany before the war. Much of what I knew or imagined about his early years was drawn from an album of old photographs, one of the few personal items he was able to bring with him when he immigrated to the United States in 1937. It was filled with pictures of elegantly dressed, confident-looking people, secure about their places in the world, posed in front of stately houses and picturesque landscapes. There was no hint of the catastrophic events that would soon envelop them and millions of other European Jews.

As a boy I spent hours leafing through the frayed pages of that album. To a middle-class kid growing up in a stiflingly dull Connecticut suburb, the pictures were a window into an exotic world. There was my father skiing in Yugoslavia, horseback riding in Italy, swimming off the Dalmatian Coast, hiking in the Bavarian hills. In every picture he is meticulously groomed, his short dark hair brushed back and mustache neatly trimmed. He is often dressed in a suit and tie, sometimes accessorized with a hat, handkerchief, and gloves. I sometimes wondered how that dashing young blade turned into the sedate, pot-bellied man I knew as my father.

The picture I liked the best showed two men dressed in fur-collared overcoats feeding the pigeons at St. Mark's Square in Venice.

One of them, wearing an impish smile under his homburg, was my grandfather Otto; the other, bare-headed and darkly handsome, a pigeon perched on his outstretched arm, was my father.

Fascinated by the world captured in those photographs, I would ply Dad with questions. Who are those people? Where was this taken? What are those mountains in the distance? Most of the time he swatted my questions away as if they were flies. If he did respond, the answers were invariably brief and maddingly vague, which only piqued my interest more.

In 1979, when I was 28, three years after my father died, I decided the time had come to satisfy my curiosity about the world he had left behind. I wanted to see the house he had lived in, walk the streets he had walked, perhaps even meet some of the people he had known. I quit my job as a proofreader at a corporate law firm in New York and purchased a round-trip flight to Europe on a discount airline ($99 each way, BYO everything). Armed with a Eurail Pass, a *Let's Go Europe* guidebook, and about $500 in traveler's checks, I spent six weeks dashing from city to city like a crazed kid in a candy store. Starting in Brussels, my itinerary included Amsterdam, Berlin, Munich, Innsbruck, Venice, Rome, Florence, Nice, and Paris. There was one other stop: Weiden, the small city in northeastern Bavaria where Dad was born and grew up.

Shortly before leaving for Europe, I went to see Frederic Alberti, the New York lawyer who had represented my father in his efforts to obtain reparations from the German government for losses his family had suffered in the Holocaust. (Dad and his brother Ernst eventually received a few thousand dollars each, but it was much less than they had hoped for.) A gaunt, elderly man with a gentle demeanor, Alberti smiled wanly as I explained the purpose of my trip. Behind him, through a window overlooking Sixth Avenue, I could see Midtown traffic crawling uptown like a procession of ants.

Alberti picked up a thick manila envelope sitting on his desk and handed it to me. "I'm not sure any of this will be very helpful," he said wearily, "but I think you should have it."

Inside I found a sheaf of old documents, including Dad's German birth certificate, driver's license, and passport, as well as the passenger list of the SS *Bremen*, the ship on which he sailed to America, dated October 19, 1937, with his name underlined in black ink. One other document caught my eye – a faded yellow form with the word *Todesfallanzeige* printed in thick capital letters at the top. It was the death certificate for my grandfather Otto, who died in Theresienstadt, a Jewish ghetto in western Czechoslovakia, on December 27, 1942.

"I wish you a good trip and success with your mission," Alberti said, as he slowly stood up and extended a brittle hand. "But don't expect too much. Forty years is a long time."

Dad and granddad in Venice, circa 1935

Dad with car circa 1930

WEIDEN IN DER OBERPFALZ

It was nearly dark by the time the overnight train from Amsterdam to Berlin crossed the border into West Germany. As I watched the shadowy landscape hurtle past my compartment window, I felt a mixture of excitement and apprehension. Here I was, at long last, in my father's homeland, the place that had formed him, but also the place where my grandfather and so many other relatives had been persecuted and sent to their deaths. Even though the war had been over for decades and Germany had long since rejoined the community of civilized nations, a faint tremor of fear rippled across my chest. *Be careful*, a voice inside my head whispered. *You never know. Some Nazis might still be lurking in the shadows waiting to shiv you.*

The Berliners I met were a cold, dour lot, a far cry from the friendly and boisterous denizens of Amsterdam. As I strolled along the city's well-scrubbed streets, I was struck by the affluence Germany had achieved out of the rubble of World War II. Although I noticed a few bomb-pocked facades, most of the buildings damaged in the war had long since been restored or replaced by shiny new ones. Parks and squares were meticulously groomed and bursting with flowers, and everyone seemed to be dressed in the latest fashions and drive a late-model car.

There were no convenient train connections between Berlin and

Weiden, so I decided to hitchhike. A couple driving to Munich dropped me off about 40 miles west of Weiden, and from there I got a lift with a pair of long-haired young men in a battered Mercedes. As we sped through the verdant Bavarian countryside, past pale adobe houses adorned with blazing boxes of geraniums, modest churches with slender, gray-capped spires, and stands of lissome birch trees, it felt as if the pictures in my father's photo album were coming to life.

As we approached Weiden my companions announced that they had to make a brief stop. We pulled off the main road and drove to an ancient-looking wood-and-mortar farmhouse. Inside I was introduced to several other young men and invited to join them in smoking a bowl of hashish. I wasn't much of a drug user, but I thought it would be impolite to decline their offer, so I took a few hits from the communal pipe. As they sat around smoking and talking, mostly in German but occasionally, in deference to their American guest, in English, I was struck by how friendly and hospitable these young Bavarians were.

It was nearly dark by the time we arrived in Weiden. It was a crisp mid-September evening, 42 years after my father had left Germany for the last time. My newfound friends dropped me off near Marktplatz, the heart of the old city, a cobbled plaza lined with gabled, pastel-colored Renaissance buildings. From there I got another ride to the local youth hostel, or *Jugendherberge*, which occupied a weathered Alpine-style house on the outskirts of town.

A stony-faced old woman greeted me at the door. "Passport!" she demanded as she thrust out her hand, palm up, and muttered something about the lateness of the hour. She confirmed my reservation and grudgingly showed me to my room, a spartan dormitory with five or six bunk beds.

As I was leaving to get dinner, Frau Sourpuss warned me to be back by the 11 p.m. curfew or I would be locked out. I walked back to town and went into the first restaurant I came to. As chance would have it, a young woman I had asked for directions earlier was having drinks with several friends and invited me to join them. Her name was Christa and with her pretty, round face framed by tight, dark curls, she reminded me of Shirley Temple playing the Swiss orphan in *Heidi*.

"So, what brings you to Weiden?" Christa asked brightly. "We don't see many American tourists here."

"I'm exploring my family history," I replied. "My father was born and grew up here."

"Ah, so he was one of the lucky ones. He managed to escape this *Dreckslöch!*" said a young man with shaggy blond hair, employing the German word for shithole, as the table erupted in laughter.

I was caught off guard by the remark and wasn't sure how to respond. "You might say that," I said, after the laughter had subsided. "My father was Jewish. He left just before the war." I paused before adding, "My grandfather wasn't so lucky."

Suddenly the table fell silent as Christa and her friends stole glances at each other. After a few awkward moments the conversation shifted to *Moonraker*, the new James Bond film playing at the local theater. There was no more talk about my family or the war.

After several rounds of Weissbier and Apfelwein and numerous *Prosts!*, Christa's friends dropped me off at the hostel shortly before the witching hour. I never did get anything to eat, but after all the drinks, which they insisted on buying me, I didn't much care.

The next morning, after a breakfast of stale rolls, hard cheese, and a few slices of mystery meat, I walked to the Altes Rathaus, the ornate Old City Hall, which stands like a medieval jewel box in the middle of Marktplatz. I was directed to the office of the *Oberbürgermeister*, or mayor, where I explained the purpose of my visit to a stern-faced young man behind the counter.

"The person in charge of such matters as family histories is not available today," he said curtly.

"But I am only planning to be in Weiden until Sunday," I explained. "Is there no one else who can help me?"

"I'm afraid not," he said with a shrug as he turned to return to his desk. "You'll have to come back on Monday."

With no better ideas, I set out to look for my grandfather Otto's old house, the stone manor that was the backdrop to several pictures in my father's photo album. Dad spoke about the house, with its gardens and stables, from time to time, and when he did a wisp of melancholia would creep into his voice. My cousin Erich Kupfer, who grew up in Munich and often visited Weiden as a child, had warned me that the house had probably been destroyed during the war. But I needed to find out for myself.

Guided by an old map, I walked south of the city center and crossed a narrow river into a leafy residential neighborhood. As I approached my grandfather's old street, my stomach began to churn with conflicting emotions. I was excited at the prospect of discovering a piece of my father's former life, but I also felt sad because, if I did find anything, it would be the remnants of a world that no longer existed. Sad, too, that Dad couldn't be with me to share the moment.

My thoughts turned to a box of old papers I had discovered in my parents' attic shortly after my father died. It contained copies of letters he had written to various government agencies, aid organizations, travel agencies, and shipping lines trying, with increasing urgency, to arrange for Otto to immigrate to the United States. It also included personal correspondence between Dad and his father and other relatives scattered across Europe, the US, and South America.

The correspondence between Dad and his father spanned seven months, from April to November 1941, a period during which Otto and his sister Hermine had been forced to sell the family home in Weiden and move to Frankfurt. Otto's letters, neatly typed on onionskin paper, often with a brief handwritten postscript from Mina (short for Hermine), reflected their growing desperation to get out of Germany.

When I turned the corner into Wiegelstrasse, I was surprised to find a swath of open space cut into the tight-knit fabric of the neighborhood, with a few newish buildings sprouting out of the dirt and weeds. A concrete multilevel garage stood blankly facing the street, across from a little roadside sausage stand, the kind that are ubiquitous in Germany. When I asked some passersby where I could find No. 19, they confirmed what Erich suspected: the street had been bombed during the war and the house likely no longer existed.

"Ask the newspaper," a young man suggested, pointing to a modern office building down the street.

Sure enough, the building was occupied by the offices of *Der Neue Tag* [The New Day], the local paper. When I explained the purpose of my visit to the receptionist, she called over a young man, apparently an editor, who took an immediate interest in my story. As word got around the office about who I was and what I was doing in Weiden, we were soon surrounded by a knot of curious onlookers. I felt a bit embarrassed by all the attention I was receiving, but after being ignored or snapped at by most of the people I had met in Berlin, I was also enjoying my newfound celebrity.

The editor escorted me into an inner office and introduced me to an attractive middle-aged woman with neatly coiffed blond hair sitting behind a desk. She stood up to greet me, revealing a tall, slender figure smartly dressed in a dark blazer and skirt and a white blouse.

"Hallo Mr. Kupfer," she said, smiling warmly as she reached across the desk and gave me a firm handshake. "A pleasure to meet you."

Her name was Inge Roegner and in halting, heavily accented English she explained that she would like to write an article about my visit. The story would ask anyone who had any information about my family to contact the newspaper and, because it would be published the next day, a Saturday, she would include her personal phone number as well.

As I was being interviewed by Frau Roegner, a man sitting nearby started tearing through the newspaper on his desk. "Kupfer!" he exclaimed as he thumped his forefinger on one of the pages. At first I thought he must be looking at an old issue he had just dug out of the morgue. But, no, the top of the page read "Freitag, 14. September 1979." It was that morning's edition.

The man was pointing to a full-page article under the headline, "*Eine Fabrik Schiesst Ihre Tore*" [A Factory Closes Its Doors]. "As of today," the article began, "the chimneys are no longer smoking" at the flat glass factory on Dr.-Seeling-Strasse, which was being replaced by a modern new complex in the nearby town of Weiherhammer. The closure marked "the end of a long chapter of glassmaking history ... [that] has defined the economic life of Weiden and the surrounding area for almost 90 years." The story was illustrated with a modern-day aerial photograph of the sprawling factory complex as well as a pair of old photos, taken around the turn of the 20th century, showing the exterior of the factory complex and workers posed in front of the foundry.

But the part of the article that had drawn the man's attention came in a paragraph two-thirds of the way down the first column. It noted that two years after the factory first opened in 1890 it was purchased by Eduard and Aloys Kupfer, a pair of businessmen who owned several other glass foundries in the region.

"Mein Gott! Ich kann es nicht glauben!" [My God! I can't believe it!] Inge exclaimed, as she looked over her colleague's shoulder. "This must be the factory your family owned before the war!"

I shook my head in dismay. My father had told me his family had been in the glass business and had owned a factory in Weiden, but beyond that I knew almost nothing. It was hard to believe that, four decades since a Kupfer last stepped foot in Weiden, the factory his family had once owned was going out of business that very afternoon. But there it was, in black and white, right in front of my eyes.

As I was absorbing this news, Inge made a call to Hermann Brenner, the longtime leader of the Jewish community in Weiden. Herr Brenner told her he was not familiar with my father's family, but he suggested I talk to a local shopkeeper named Lothar Friedmann, one of only two Jewish residents of Weiden who had returned to the city after the war. Most of the other former Jewish residents, like my father and grandfather, had either fled the country or been murdered in the camps. The city's small Jewish population now consisted almost entirely of Eastern Europeans who had settled in Weiden after the war.

That afternoon I went to see Herr Friedmann at his men's clothing store on Marktplatz. A short, round-faced man dressed in a rumpled sports coat and a button-down shirt that hung loosely around his bulging waist, he reminded me of the legions of elderly

Jewish men trundling around my neighborhood on the Upper West Side of Manhattan. Although I couldn't understand his words, the sing-song inflections of his voice and his self-effacing manner were familiar. Unfortunately, he didn't know my family, or at least had no memory of them. As his wife told me, shaking her head plaintively: "It's been a long time."

Late that afternoon I walked over to the factory to take a look around. I followed the railroad tracks southwest of the city center to a complex of soot-stained brick buildings punctuated by a pair of towering smokestacks. A sign outside the main building read, "Flachglas AG."

As I approached the entrance a burly, bald-headed man was pulling shut a heavy iron gate, about to close the factory for the day and, if the article in *Der Neue Tag* was correct, for the last time. I called out to him, waving the newspaper in the air.

"*Dies ist das?*" I asked, employing my piddling German, as I pointed to the article about the factory.

He squinted his eyes suspiciously and nodded.

"I am a Kupfer," I said. "My *Grossvater* was *Direktor* here."

The man obviously didn't speak English but when I mentioned the name Kupfer his head tilted.

"*Kupfer. Sie Kupfer?*" he asked, skeptically.

"*Ja, ja!*" I said, nodding vigorously.

After a moment he flapped his hand impatiently, gesturing for me to come inside, and slammed the gate shut behind me. I followed him up a steep flight of stairs and down a long, narrow corridor. We entered an office where several men were standing around talking. The bald guy explained who I was to the others. There was a brief discussion and then a tall, thick-necked man with blond hair and flinty blue eyes gestured for me to follow him.

He led me down the hall into a large conference room. There, seated around a long, rectangular table cluttered with beer bottles, half-filled glasses, and smoldering ashtrays was a group of about a dozen mostly elderly men dressed in jackets and ties. There was something frightening about these men with their gray hair, weathered faces, and dour expressions. In my excited state, I felt as if

I had just walked into a scene from an old war movie and these men – these Nazis! – were plotting their next acts of destruction.

The blond whispered into the ear of a younger, dark-haired man seated at the center of the table. After a few moments the man stood up and approached me, holding out his hand. "Mr. Kupfer," he said, smiling.

The sound of my father's name in that room sent a shiver up my spine. He introduced himself as Sepp Hummel, the director of the factory, and asked me a few questions in perfect English. *Where was I from? What was I doing in Weiden?* I showed him some old photographs of my father and grandfather that I had brought with me. He studied the pictures and nodded, apparently in no hurry to resume the meeting.

As I chatted with Herr Hummel I heard my father's name ricochet around the room. Out of the corner of my eye I could see the other men looking at me suspiciously, as if I were an imposter or an apparition.

After a few minutes, the director motioned for me to take a seat at the end of the table and began his presentation. Although I could understand little of what he was saying, he was evidently discussing the history of the company and the evolution of the technology used to manufacture sheet glass.

A series of aerial photographs of different factories hung on the opposite wall and, one by one, Herr Hummel pointed to the pictures and made a few remarks. Finally, he came to a larger picture that stood alone on a wall at the far end of the room. This was the Weiden *Glasfabrik*. The closure of the factory, after almost 90 years, was a "meaningful hour," he noted, because of its importance to the local economy and the glassmaking industry in the region. As the director discussed the history of the factory, he mentioned the name Kupfer several times, and each time that he did he gestured toward me and smiled.

After Hummel concluded his remarks, the meeting was opened for a general discussion. The atmosphere became more relaxed as the men sipped beer, smoked, and chatted. They smiled and laughed as they exchanged toasts and shared stories about the old days at the factory. Then they gathered in front of the picture of the Weiden factory for a group photograph.

I sat there in stunned silence. Less than 24 hours earlier I had arrived in my father's hometown not knowing whether I would find even a scrap of information about his family. Now here I was attending the final meeting of the factory his family had once owned, surrounded by men who not only had worked there but may have known my father and grandfather.

Once again my thoughts drifted to the box of old letters I found in my parents' attic. Early in the correspondence between Dad and his father, Otto and his sister seemed hopeful that he would join his son in America one day. "Your reunion with father will soon get serious," Mina wrote in April 1941. But a few weeks later, after recounting a series of setbacks in his efforts to secure safe passage through Portugal, Otto sounded less than confident: "It will certainly be very difficult but one must not give up hope. ... In the end everyone will surely have their turn." He noted that he is studying cooking and English in preparation for joining his son, though he confessed he wasn't doing very well with the latter. "It is very difficult to get it into an old head," he lamented.

As conditions worsened, Otto's tone shifted to frustration and despair. In late September, he revealed that he had lost 40 pounds and warned his son: "If we ever are lucky enough to see each other again, you will meet a scrawny man." Two weeks later he wrote, "Let's hope for the best. There's nothing else we can do." And in a postcard on November 15, in one of his last communications with his son, he noted: "I just wanted to let you know that we are still alive."

After the meeting broke up, I passed around some old photos of my father and grandfather that I had taken from Dad's album. Several men nodded in recognition. One elderly gentleman with a rutted face, bulbous nose, and thick mane of white hair looked me straight in the eye. "You look like a Kupfer," he said.

Hearing those words, linking me so directly to my German ancestors, made my bones tingle with pride. Yes, this was really happening. I wasn't imagining it.

The man's name was Fritz Wallner. He told me he had worked at the factory his entire life. Indeed, he was one of the boys in the photograph of the factory workers that appeared in the morning paper. That picture had been taken 83 years earlier, which made Herr Wallner 90 if a day.

Another elderly man, Wilhelm Ludwigs, said he remembered my grandfather and his family well. Ludwigs, who insisted I call him Willi, invited me to his home Sunday afternoon and promised to ask other former workers from the factory to join us.

On Monday morning a photograph appeared in *Der Neue Tag* showing Herr Hummel addressing the meeting. To the director's right, at the far end of the table, the head of the former owner's grandson was barely visible.

"There are workers here from the early days who experienced the switch from glassblowing by mouth to the mechanical drawing process in 1928," the caption noted. "Now, after 50 years, this method of production is ending too as the industry shifts to the 'float glass' process.[1]

"Past and present are meeting in another way," the caption continued. "As chance would have it, Peter Cooper joined the conversation. The 28-year-old New Yorker was following the footsteps of his German ancestors, among whom were Aloys and Eduard Kupfer, who in 1892 took over the glass factory in Weiden."

Weiden Glashütte, early 1900s

Postcard Marktplatz Weiden, 1930s

Frankenreuth glass foundry, circa 1908

Otto Kupfer and cow, circa 1930

Otto Kupfer, mid-1930s

Otto Kupfer, mid-1930s

Death Certificate Otto Theresienstadt

'THE LORDS ARE COMING'

On Saturday morning, as Inge had promised, an article about my visit appeared in *Der Neue Tag*. The headline read: "*Gesucht: Freunde der Familie Kupfer / Junger Amerikaner Forscht Vorfahren – Vater in Weiden Geboren.*" [Wanted: Friends of the Kupfer family / Young American Researches Jewish Ancestry – Father Born in Weiden.].

The story was accompanied by one of the photographs from Dad's album showing a group of people gathered around a table in front of a house with decoratively carved stone walls and columns and ornate leaded windows. On the far right, my grandfather Otto, dapperly dressed in a vested suit and bowtie, a handkerchief tucked in his breast pocket, was leaning forward in his chair, hands crossed on his lap, looking intently at the camera. A boy of five or six, dressed in lederhosen and boots, sat with his elbow resting on the table, smiling sweetly. That was my cousin Erich.[1]

When I got back to the hostel on Saturday afternoon, grumpy *Greisin* informed me that a man named Eduard Wittmann had called. When I returned the call, Herr Wittmann explained that he had read Inge's article with great interest because his family had also been in the glass business and had known the Kupfers. The Wittmanns had run a *Schleif und Polierwerken* [a glass grinding and polishing mill] and most of the raw glass for their operation had been supplied by the Kupfer foundry in Weiden.

Wittmann invited me to join him the following day to attend a church festival in the nearby town of Pleystein and have dinner afterward at his father Karl's house. I wasn't so keen about the church part but was thrilled at the prospect of meeting a former associate of my grandfather, so I eagerly accepted.

The next morning Wittmann picked me up promptly at 9 a.m. in a gleaming white Mercedes. He was a middle-aged man with a fringe of gray hair at the base of his large head, a ruddy complexion, and a wide, gap-toothed smile. He was casually dressed in a shirt, slacks, and a traditional Bavarian-style jacket with a rounded collar and decorative buttons.

It was a glorious autumn day, warm and sunny, with just a hint of crispness in the air. Eddie, as he insisted I call him, was a gregarious man and, fortunately for me, spoke excellent English. As we raced through the rolling hills of the Bavarian countryside, he expounded on the history of the glass industry in the Oberpfalz, as this part of Bavaria was called, shouting to be heard above the wind whistling through the open windows.

The Oberpfalz has long been a center for glassmaking, he explained, and the Kupfer family had played a significant role in that history. In addition to the factory in Weiden, the Kupfers and their business partners had owned several other glass factories in the area, including one in Fürth, a city outside of Nuremburg known for making mirror glass. The family's first glass foundry, reputed to be the oldest in the Oberpfalz, was in Frankenreuth, a hamlet on the Czech border where my grandfather was born and raised.

As I listened to Herr Wittmann discourse on the history of glassmaking in the region and the Kupfers' contribution to that history, I couldn't help but feel a swell of pride. What had been a vague picture of a successful family business, in my father's telling, was coming into sharper focus. My grandfather had run one of the largest companies in the area and had been a prominent member of the community. What must he have felt, I wondered, to have all that stripped away, to find himself and his sister helpless and alone, with no one to turn to, as the walls of Nazi persecution closed in on them.

Eddie was obviously proud of the Oberpfalz and its people. He would occasionally interrupt his history lesson to comment on a local site or wave to people we passed on the road, and they would invariably return the greeting. Clearly, he and his big white Mercedes were well known in the area.

Pleystein was a picture postcard of a town with crooked little streets lined with white and yellow stucco houses garnished with colorful flower boxes. Everything was so clean and tidy it looked like a stage set. The town was buzzing with activity in preparation for the annual festival. Banners flapped in the breeze as villagers dressed in their Sunday best, children in tow, made their way to the church.

We parked in the center of town and climbed a rocky hill crowned by an imposing neo-Baroque church. Several hundred people had gathered outside the austere church, beneath a soaring bell tower, for the open-air service. Most of the worshippers appeared to be simple, working-class folks. The men tended to have long faces, prominent noses, thin lips and straight, slicked-back hair; the women wore plain dresses with shawls draped over their heads and shoulders. Although Transylvania was hundreds of miles to the east, I couldn't help thinking of the villagers in the Frankenstein movies.

I soon learned it wasn't just the festival or the picturesque setting that had brought us to Pleystein. Eddie nodded toward the white-robed pastor leading the service. "That's my brother," he said matter-of-factly.

After the service Eddie gave me a tour of the interior of the church, a small but sumptuous space decorated with ornate carvings and colorful frescoes. He pointed to a plaque on the wall honoring the 15th-century founders, which included several of his ancestors. "So you see," he said with a wry smile, "we Wittmanns have been here for a long time."

Then we walked back down the hill where the festival was in full swing. The main street was lined with stalls offering a bounty of breads, cakes, sausages, and other regional fare. The sparkling fall weather seemed to put everyone in a festive mood. People smiled and nodded to each other as they strolled among the booths.

Eddie, who appeared to know everyone, stopped to chat every few minutes, and each time he did he would introduce me and explain who I was. We went into a shop where he bought me a little book on the history of the Oberpfalz. When I picked out a few postcards to send home he insisted on buying those too.

Then we drove to his father's house, a beautifully preserved 14th-century farmhouse on the outskirts of town. Inside I was greeted by a flock of family members, including Karl, the 84-year-old patriarch, and two of Eduard's brothers along with their wives and children. Everyone greeted me politely, but no one made much of an effort to communicate beyond that. I assumed that was because they didn't speak English well and preferred to leave the talking to Eddie.

Karl Wittmann was a frail man with a pencil-thin mustache who walked with the aid of a cane. He was dressed in a dark Bavarian-style suit with narrow lapels and a string bowtie. Communicating with him was difficult. On top of the language barrier, his hearing wasn't good and he was also distracted, understandably, by the presence of his family. So I didn't learn as much about my father's family as I had hoped. But one thing became clear: Karl and my grandfather had been more than just business associates; they had also been friends who had visited each other's homes.

I couldn't help wondering how much Karl knew about what had happened to the Kupfers and the other Jewish families in the area under the Nazis. Surely he had heard that Otto and Mina had been forced to sell their house in Weiden and move to Frankfurt. Did he also know that they had been deported to a concentration camp? Did he know they had been murdered? And if he did, what, if anything, had he done to try to help them?

I never learned the answers to those questions, but Eddie later told me something that offered a clue. Toward the end of the war his grandfather Josef, Karl's father, allowed a Polish Jew to hide in their factory for several months. It was an act of considerable courage because, had the man been discovered by the authorities, Josef and his entire family would almost certainly have been arrested. After the Allied invasion, the man left and they never heard from him again.

Eduard and Karl took me on a brief tour of the long-abandoned glass finishing works, which stood a short distance from the house. It consisted of two long, narrow sheds separated by a dry canal. Eddie explained how water flowing through the canal would turn a large wheel outside each shed to power the flattening and polishing machines. The Wittmanns' business thrived for generations, he said, but changes in sheet glass production methods eventually rendered it obsolete. Eddie was now in the porcelain business, another important industry in the Oberpfalz.

Before dinner, we joined hands for a brief prayer. And what a dinner it was: platters heaped with roast duck, red cabbage salad and Knödel – baseball-sized but surprisingly light potato dumplings, the kind Dad hankered for but Mom could never quite master – washed down with plenty of Weissbier.

After dinner Eddie and one of his nephews took me upstairs to a room that was essentially a family museum, filled with relics of the Wittmanns' long history in the Oberpfalz. Eddie unfurled a dusty scroll with French script. "This is a legal document from Napoleon's time. It spells out property rights passed down from father to son," he explained. "And here is our family coat of arms," his nephew chimed in, pointing to a large wooden shield, its multi-colored paint cracked and faded, leaning haphazardly again a massive hand-carved chest.

Coming from a country barely 200 years old, I was fascinated by this trove of family memorabilia. I could think of only one heirloom in my family of any note, a brass samovar my mother's parents brought over from Ukraine at the beginning of the 20th century, which was proudly displayed on a pedestal table in my parents' living room and now holds a prominent place in mine.

We took a few photographs in front of the farmhouse before Eduard and I set off for Frankenreuth, five miles to the east. A speck on the map near the ancient market town of Waidhaus, the entire settlement consisted of a few roads and a couple of dozen buildings. Only a small yellow marker by the side of the road prevented us from speeding past it into Czechoslovakia.

Eduard blithely banged on the door of the first house we came to and called out a greeting. A young man came to the door and directed us to another house down the road. The house was not much bigger than a shack, with a tidy little garden enclosed by a rickety post-and-rail fence. A printed sign attached to the fence read, "A. Dobner."

Eduard pounded on the door and, not bothering to wait for a response, walked right in. If he had done that in the United States, I couldn't help thinking, he stood a good chance of getting shot, but in rural Bavaria this was apparently considered acceptable behavior. We found ourselves in a small, dark room stippled by bright afternoon sunlight streaming in through the window. A cast iron wood-burning stove stood against the rear wall and a few kitchen utensils hung from pegs on the wall.

It took me a moment to realize that there were three people sitting around a small wooden table by the window. An old man with a bushy yellowish mustache, dressed in a faded plaid shirt and suspenders, sat nearest the door. A cigarette was wedged between his fingers and a glass of amber-colored beer stood on the table in front of him. Across from him, on the far side of the table, a middle-aged woman gazed at us silently as she took a long drag on her cigarette. Between them, facing the window, sat an older woman with tousled gray hair. None of them seemed the least bit surprised that two strangers had just barged into their kitchen uninvited.

Eduard introduced himself and his American sidekick. When he mentioned the name Kupfer, the old man's face lit up. Yes, he knew my family, knew them well. Like almost everyone else in Frankenreuth, he had worked at the glass foundry. Not only that, his aunt had been a housekeeper in the Kupfers' house.

His name was Adam Dobner, the woman next to him was his wife, Hermine, and the younger woman was their daughter. When I showed Herr Dobner the photograph of the Kupfer clan gathered at my grandfather's house in Weiden – a picture taken half a century earlier – he nodded and picked out Otto without a moment's hesitation. Hermine also recognized my grandfather from the photo.

Once again I found myself in a state of disbelief. Here I was in a remote Bavarian hamlet I hadn't even heard of until the day before talking to a man who not only knew my father's family but had worked for them for many years.

Speaking in short bursts interrupted by gasping breaths, Dobner talked at length about the old days at the *Glashütte*. He seemed just as excited to be reliving that history as I was to be hearing it for the first time. As Eddie translated for me, I madly scribbled notes in my travel diary.

When Adam first began working at the foundry as a young man he lived across the border in Czechoslovakia, in an area largely inhabited by ethnic Germans called Sudetenland. He was employed as a mechanic, building and repairing machinery. He later moved into the house we were sitting in, next door to the foundry, which was now largely dismantled.

With his gnarled, nicotine-stained fingers jabbing the air for emphasis, he described how the glassworks was laid out and operated as Eduard sketched diagrams on a sheet of paper. First a mixture of sand and potash was melted in a large furnace fueled by trees from the surrounding forest. Then the workers used long pipes to blow the molten glass into balloons. After the hollow orbs cooled, they were cut and flattened at a nearby grinding and polishing mill, like the one Eddie's family had owned.

"The workers had to be very strong because they had to dance around to make sure the glass stayed round," Dobner recalled. With that, he stood up and did a little jig as his hands formed a cylinder in front of his mouth. "We drank a lot of beer because it was hot as hell inside the foundry. That's why Bavarian glass often smelled of beer," he added, giggling like a teenager.

The workers were treated fairly and paid well, Dobner said. He earned 500 to 600 marks a month, which was considered good money in those days, though he had to pay his assistants out of that pot. But relations between owners and workers took a fractious turn in the mid-1920s, when hyperinflation caused the German mark to become virtually worthless and a week's pay was barely enough to purchase a pound of meat.[2] The workers demanded to be paid in Czech kroners, and when my grandfather refused, they went on strike. The dispute was settled when Otto agreed to pay the workers in US dollars, a relatively strong currency at the time.

In addition to the foundry, Dobner said, the Kupfers owned a considerable amount of other property in the area, including several houses, a brewery, and large tracts of forest and farmland. After the family moved to Weiden, they would return to Frankenreuth periodically to check on the *Glashütte* and their other properties. Not many people owned automobiles in those days, so when the workers saw the Kupfers driving down the road, "we knew the Lords were coming," he said with a snort.

After chatting for an hour or so in the Dobners' tiny kitchen we went outside to take some pictures. Then we walked up the road to the site of the old foundry. All that remained was a large barnlike structure sitting in an overgrown field. We got back in the car and drove a short distance in the opposite direction to a small pink stucco building with a peaked roof and steeple and a large crucifix above the entryway. This was the workers' chapel, which I later learned was built by the original owners of the foundry and restored by the Kupfers after they acquired the property in the 1860s.

Farther down the road stood a sprawling white stucco house enclosed on three sides by stables. This was Frankenreuth No. 1, the manor house where my grandfather and his 11 siblings grew up. The locals called it the *Schloss* [castle], Dobner said. Once again I felt a flicker of pride knowing the prominent place my family had once occupied in the community – albeit a very, very small community – but also a sense of unease knowing the darkness that would come.

On the way back to Weiden, we pulled up to a gas pump by the side of the road attended by an elderly gentleman in a cardigan. As Eddie explained, with typical aplomb, who I was and what we were doing in Frankenreuth, the man's face brightened. His name was Johann Herold, he told us, he had lived in Frankenreuth his entire life and he, too, remembered my father's family.

Herr Herold confirmed much of what Adam Dobner had told us. The Kupfers had a good relationship with the foundry workers, most of whom were Catholic, he said. Besides maintaining the chapel, the owners had installed a large cross inside the foundry itself. They also built a small synagogue in the manor house, where Jews from around the area would gather to pray.

By the time we got back to Weiden I was an hour late for my appointment with Willi Ludwigs, who lived in an apartment building down the street from the glass factory. No one answered the door but, as often happened during my visit, disappointment was quickly followed by good fortune. As Eddie was writing a note to apologize for being late, we met another resident of the building whose mother and husband had both worked at the glass foundry and had known the Kupfers. As it turned out, the husband was Fritz Wallner, another one of the men I had met at the factory on Friday afternoon.

We followed Frau Wallner downstairs into her cramped, dimly lit kitchen. She introduced us to her mother, a small, shriveled woman named Katharina Anzer. When I showed Frau Anzer a photograph of my grandfather she immediately nodded in recognition.

Katharina began working at the factory when she was 25, sweeping up pieces of broken glass, and it was there that she met her husband. "It was terribly hot inside the foundry," she recalled, fanning her face with her hand by way of illustration. "Everyone wore white uniforms" to deflect the intense heat.

While we were talking to Katharina and her daughter, Fritz Wallner and several other family members walked in. A handsome man with a gray pompadour and a gentle demeanor, Wallner had worked at the Weiden foundry all his life, as had his father before him. He picked up a copy of *Der Neue Tag* that was lying on the kitchen table and pointed to the old photo showing workers posed in front of the foundry. "That's me!" he said, tapping his forefinger at a boy no older than seven or eight sitting cross-legged on the ground.

As we sipped glasses of malty Dunkelweizen and smoked my Marlboros, Herr Wallner recalled the old days at the factory while the others smiled and laughed, occasionally chiming in with comments of their own. "We felt fortunate to work there because we were well paid and the benefits were good," he said. "There was even a sick fund for employees," which was not common in those days.

"The owners made sure the workers were well taken care of," Katharina added. "There was a slaughterhouse and a butcher, a canteen, even a bakery. They built a large assembly hall for dances and other social events, and your grandfather always made a point of stopping by."

The Kupfers had built the apartment building we were in as well as several others on the street, Fritz noted, waving his arm around the kitchen. "We paid only a few marks a month in rent, which included the coal to heat the buildings." Now, like many other residents of the building, he and his wife and mother-in-law were retired and living on a pension provided by the company.

My grandfather lived down the street from the factory in a large house surrounded by flowers and fruit trees, Wallner recalled. Every day he would walk through his garden on his way to and from work. As a young man, Fritz admitted, he would sometimes reach over the fence and pick a piece of the boss's fruit. The belated confession elicited a crackle of laughter in the crowded kitchen.

Wallner remembered my grandfather as a kind man who seemed genuinely concerned about the welfare of his workers, but he was also a tough taskmaster who demanded respect. "When Herr Kupfer came to inspect the factory floor, the workers were expected to line up military style," he said with a wry smile. The workers were not allowed to smoke in the foundry because the furnaces were powered by gas, but one day the boss caught Fritz having a cigarette and reprimanded him, he recalled with a chuckle.

As they sat around the kitchen table reminiscing about the old days at the factory, I was struck by how warm and down-to-earth these Weideners were. They were proud of their work, proud of their city, proud of their Bavarian heritage. Gathering in each other's kitchens to drink beer, smoke, and shoot the breeze was obviously a popular pastime.

But when the conversation turned to the Nazi era and what happened to the Kupfers and the other Jewish families, as I made sure it did, the atmosphere grew a little less warm. "We had a good relationship with the Kupfers and the other Jewish families," Wallner insisted, shaking his head dolefully. "It was the government that created the problems." As for the concentration camps, his response was one I heard often during my visit: "We didn't know what was happening. We thought the camps were for common criminals – Jews and non-Jews alike."

After an hour or so we adjourned outside to take pictures. Then Eddie, who seemed to have a boundless store of energy, offered to take me to a museum of glassmaking near Regensburg, the capital of the Oberpfalz, about 50 miles south of Weiden. At first I demurred, not wanting to take up any more of his time, but when he said he was going there anyway to pick up his wife, who was returning from a vacation in South Africa, I agreed to join him.

By the time we arrived at the museum it was already closed, but Eddie described the exhibits as we peered through the windows. Then he gunned his Mercedes up a narrow, winding road (Germans, I discovered, love to drive fast) to his brother-in-law's house on a hillside overlooking the city. As it turned out, his wife's flight had been delayed and she wouldn't be arriving until the next day, so we drove back to town and Eddie treated me to a traditional Bavarian supper of potato soup, steak with mustard sauce, and Hefeweisen in a historic half-timbered restaurant in the city center. Then we drove to his house, a centuries-old manor in the hamlet of Gut Grub. Surrounded by old paintings and kitschy (but no doubt expensive) furniture, we capped our meal with a homemade apple tart and sweet, syrupy German wine.

After dessert Eduard suggested I call my mother in the States. At first I declined, not wanting to take advantage of his hospitality, but he insisted. Mom was thrilled to hear my voice, especially because it was our first communication since I had left for Europe two weeks earlier. (Email had yet to be invented and international phone calls cost a fortune.) I quickly filled her in on my action-packed visit to Weiden, but her main concern seemed to be my caloric intake. "Are you eating enough?" she asked. I almost laughed at the question because that was the least of my concerns. It had taken only a few days in Bavaria to understand why Dad was so fond of hearty meals freighted with meat, potatoes, and rich desserts.

Eddie dropped me off at the hostel just before the 11 p.m. curfew. I was exhausted but full of gratitude after one of the most memorable days of my trip, if not my life.

The Manor house in Frankenreuth around 1900

CONFUSION AT THE CEMETERY

On Monday morning I went back to the offices of *Der Neue Tag* to see Inge. "I have some exciting news!" she announced. She had received several phone calls over the weekend from people who had read her article and remembered Dad's family. One family in Fürth offered to take me to the city archives, where they were certain I would find information about the Kupfers. Hermann Brenner, the Jewish community leader, also called and offered to help me in my quest. In fact, Inge said, his son was on his way to see me at that very moment.

A few minutes later Hardy Brenner, a handsome young man with intense blue eyes, and his pretty, raven-haired girlfriend, Gabi, walked into Inge's office. Gabi showed me copies of some documents about the Kupfers she had obtained from the municipal archives for a university project she had done on the Jewish community. One document in particular caught my eye: It listed the name, birthdate, and place of birth – all Frankenreuth – of Otto and his 11 brothers and sisters. In some cases, it also indicated who and when they married and when and where they died.

When I expressed surprise at the size of my grandfather's family, Gabi said I shouldn't be. Large families were not unusual in those days, she explained, because disease claimed the lives of nearly one in three children before the age of one.

And why did she happen to have so much information about my father's family, I wondered. That, too, should come as no surprise, she said, because Weiden had a small Jewish community – fewer than 200 Jews lived in the city before the war – and the Kupfers were regarded as one of the most important Jewish families in town.

Hardy and Gabi offered to drive me to the Jewish cemetery to see if any Kupfers were buried there. I knew Otto had died in Theresienstadt and his sister Mina had suffered the same fate in Treblinka, in occupied Poland, so I assumed their remains weren't in Weiden. Dad's older brother, Ernst, had immigrated to France in 1933, several years before Dad fled to the US. But perhaps his mother, Berta, who died long before the war, and other relatives were buried in Weiden.

As we were about to leave for the cemetery, Inge's phone rang. It was Christina Gottshall, an elderly woman I had met earlier who lived around the corner from the newspaper office. She told Inge she had some information about my family and was coming to her office straight away to give it to me.

I will never forget the scene that greeted us as we stepped outside. A frail old woman was hobbling down the street waving a piece of paper.

"Herr Kupfer! Herr Kupfer!" she gasped as she came up to me and thrust the paper into my hand. Speaking in short bursts as Inge translated, she explained that she had spoken to several friends who remembered Dad's family and had written down their names and phone numbers.

"You must call them right away," she said, cupping my hand in her boney fingers. "I'm sure you will find some news about your family."

She herself remembered my father from her schooldays. "He was so handsome," she recalled with a shy smile. "All the girls thought he was a good catch."

As she stood there trying to catch her breath, I gave her a gentle hug. "*Dankeschön!*" I said.

"*Nein, nein,*" she replied, shaking her head. "*Schon gut.*" [It's nothing.].

The cemetery occupied a small patch of land tucked away behind a locked metal gate in a residential neighborhood. As we wandered among the well-tended plots, Hardy spotted a newish-looking pinkish-gray tombstone toward the rear of the cemetery with the name Kupfer engraved in gold. There were no other markings; no first names, no dates, no epitaphs.

As I gazed silently at what was almost certainly the grave of my ancestors, I felt my body stiffen and the hairs on the back of my neck tingle. Who was buried here, I wondered. My grandmother Berta? My great grandparents Eduard and Franziska? And if not them, who? After a few minutes, following the Jewish custom, I picked up a small rock, placed it on the headstone, and said a silent prayer.

I was surprised that the gravesite was in such good shape considering that so many years had passed since a member of my family had been in Weiden. Hardy and Gabi explained that the cemetery had been vandalized during the Nazi era, most likely on *Kristallnacht,* the infamous Night of Broken Glass, and rebuilt after the war by the Jewish community. But there was no way of knowing exactly who was buried where because many of the headstones had been overturned and smashed and the cemetery records destroyed.[1] That explained why the Kupfer tombstone bore only a surname, with no first names or dates.

It was only later, after I returned home and re-examined my father's photo album, that I learned the truth. It contains photographs of two headstones: one, a large, peaked slab embellished with carved wreaths, is engraved:

Kommerzienrat
Eduard Kupfer
1840-1907

This was my great-grandfather, who held the honorary title of *Kommerzienrat*, bestowed by the Bavarian government on distinguished businessmen. Beneath Eduard's name the capital letter "F" is visible, but the rest of the name is obscured by shrubbery. This, no doubt, was Eduard's wife Franziska, or Fanni, who died in 1924.

The second headstone is inscribed:

Familie
Otto Kupfer

Below that, in smaller letters, is the name of Otto's wife Berta, my grandmother, who was only 40 when she died of cancer in 1923.

After lunch at Eddie's house we drove to Floss, an old market town about 10 miles northeast of Weiden that had been home to one of the oldest Jewish communities in Bavaria. Until the mid-19th century, Floss was one of only a few municipalities in the Oberpfalz where Jews were allowed to live. On Kristallnacht the synagogue, built in 1817, was torched and nearly burned to the ground, and the rabbi's house and Jewish community center were ransacked. No Jews returned after the war. The town has another dubious distinction: it was the birthplace of Richard Baer, an SS major who became the commandant of Auschwitz.[2]

Our first stop was the Jewish cemetery, which spilled across a tree-lined hillside on the outskirts of town. We entered through a rusted iron gate and looked around among the pocked and crumbling tombstones, some dating to the 1600s. Looking forlorn and forgotten, they leaned this way and that, as if a strong wind might topple them at any moment. The inscriptions, some in German, others in Hebrew, were so weathered they were often impossible to read. A newer section of the cemetery contained the graves of 33 victims of a Nazi concentration camp in neighboring Flossenbürg.

Finding no Kupfers among the dead, we drove to Flossenbürg, which, like many other Nazi camps, has been preserved as a memorial to its victims. Between 1938 and 1945, nearly 100,000 prisoners passed through Flossenbürg and its 100 or so subcamps.

Nearly one-third of them died from malnutrition, overwork, execution, or suicide.[3] Others died during so-called death marches they were forced to undertake as Allied forces closed in toward the end of the war.

Carved out of a tranquil wooded area near a picturesque medieval village, the site was deliberately chosen so the prisoners could be deployed as slave laborers at a nearby granite quarry. It was no coincidence that the quarry was owned by the mayor of the village, a Nazi loyalist.

This was my first visit to a concentration camp and, not surprisingly, it was the most disturbing chapter of my trip. Of course I had read stories and seen old newsreels about the camps, but nothing prepared me for the searing experience of actually visiting one. From the moment we walked through the granite gateposts, past a plaque bearing the infamous slogan *Arbeit Macht Frei* [Work sets you free], I felt slightly nauseous and light-headed, a feeling that lingered for hours after we left. The incongruity between the parklike setting and the barbarity of what went on within only added to the unsettling experience.

A cream-colored building that once served as the camp laundry was now a museum documenting the incredible cruelty meted out by Flossenbürg's administrators. We viewed the all-too-familiar pictures of emaciated prisoners staring at the camera with blank faces and hollow eyes. One document detailed the meager daily rations allotted to prisoners – soup with a single slice of bread for lunch and dinner – which were further reduced by guards who took food intended for the inmates to fatten their own bellies. I thought about my grandfather's letter complaining that he was losing weight. *If we ever are lucky enough to see each other again, you will meet a scrawny man.*

We walked to a fenced-in area below a granite watchtower, where a chute had been cut into the ground so the corpses of prisoners could be efficiently funneled into the crematorium below. Then we walked down a set of steps to the crematorium itself, a square, squat building with a tall brick chimney.

As Eddie and the others waited outside, I stepped through the doorway cut into the thick concrete walls. I found myself in a small, shadowy room illuminated by a single rectangular window set high in one wall. Even though it was a warm autumn day, it felt cool inside. A large brick oven stood impassively in one corner, its metal doors splayed open as if waiting to receive yet another body. Across from the oven stood a metal "dissecting" table where gold teeth were extracted from the bodies before they were incinerated.[4] Dozens of bodies were consumed in the oven each day, but during peak periods, as the corpses stacked up, the SS began burning them outside with gasoline. As I silently contemplated the grisly scene a sudden chill swept through my body. My arms and legs felt as stiff and heavy as the branches of the beech tree overhanging the building.

After a few minutes I rejoined the others and we followed a path to a secluded hillside called *Tal des Todes* [Valley of Death]. It was here that the SS carried out mass executions of prisoners who were no longer capable of working in the quarry and refused to die on their own. Granite slabs, each engraved with the name of a group victimized at the camp and the number of its dead, lined the ground. I slowly walked from stone to stone, studying the grim statistics. I had assumed that most of the victims of the camp were Jewish, but they were in fact only a small minority. Of the 30,000 people who died at Flossenbürg, 3,500 were Jews; the others were Poles, Czechs, Russians, French, English, Americans, Roma, political dissidents, and homosexuals, among others.

Gay men were a favorite target of the SS guards, who considered it great sport to taunt and torture them. According to one prisoner's account, the camp commander made a habit of masturbating in his pants as he watched homosexual prisoners being flogged. Others reported seeing gay men being beaten to death, having their testicles immersed alternately in hot and icy water, and having a broomstick shoved up their anus.[5]

Our last stop of the day was the municipal museum in Weiden, which occupied a beautifully restored Renaissance building near the Altes Rathaus. The city archivist, a pleasant but officious middle-aged woman named Annemarie Krauss, had been expecting us and pulled out some documents from a folder sitting on her desk – birth certificates, registration forms, and other papers about Dad's family, as well as several old photographs.

One picture in particular caught my eye: a photo of the stone manor that appeared in Dad's album. Throughout my visit to Weiden, I had received conflicting information about where his family had lived and what had become of their property. Part of the problem was that many streets had been renamed after the war. Adding to the confusion, a new system of street numbering had been adopted in Germany in the early-1930s.

Frau Krauss cleared up the mystery. "Your family had several residences in Weiden," she explained. "This house," she said, pointing to the photo of the stone manor, "was located across from the railroad station and down the street from the *Glasfabrik*. Your great grandfather Eduard purchased it in 1900 when he and his family moved to Weiden from Frankenreuth. It was known in town as the Kupfer villa."

The Weigelstrasse address was an apartment my grandfather Otto had rented after he got married. My father lived there with his parents and brother from 1912, when he was six, until 1922, when he graduated from high school and moved to Dusseldorf to take a job as an apprentice. Otto moved back to the villa in the mid-1920s, after his wife and parents had died. "Both the villa and the house on Weigelstrasse were destroyed by the American Army in the final days of the war," the archivist noted, without a hint of irony.

On Tuesday morning, my last day in Weiden, armed with the photograph of the Kupfer villa Frau Kraus had given me, I walked to the railroad station. Sure enough, the site where the stone manor had once stood, across the street, was now an asphalt parking lot. The house next door, which was also visible in the photo, was occupied by a travel agency.

I walked into the agency and introduced myself to the manager, a slender middle-aged man with a neatly trimmed mustache. I knew it was a long shot, but I had to ask: "Do you happen to remember the house that stood next door? My grandfather lived there before the war."

The manager's eyebrows arched. "Yes, of course I do! My family lived here, in this house, for many years, and the Kupfers were their neighbors. I remember the day your grandfather's house was bombed."

"You can see it there," he said, as he turned and pointed to a large oil painting hanging on the wall behind his desk. The picture showed the exterior of the building we were standing in. Next door, clearly visible in the painting, were the distinctive carved walls and leaded windows of my grandfather's house.

What the manager didn't mention – and what I didn't learn until many years later, when I was doing research for this book – was that his family had purchased the villa in 1939 after my grandfather had been forced to sell the house under the Nazi policy of *Arisierung* [Aryanization], which mandated the transfer of all Jewish-owned property in Germany to non-Jews.

I thanked the manager for his help and walked back to Inge's office to say goodbye. She was writing one last article about my visit, summing up the results of my search and describing my feelings about my time in Weiden.

As she drove me to the train station, Inge recalled the day in April 1945 that the American Army attacked Weiden. She was just a little girl, but she has never forgotten the terrifying sound of artillery fire raining down on the city.[6] Then she dropped another bombshell: after the Nazis forced my grandfather to sell the villa, party officials had occupied the house and turned it into *Kreisleitung Weiden*, their regional headquarters. The top-ranking Nazi official there, Kreisleiter Franz Bacherl, was later convicted in Nuremberg and hung.

Of all the nuggets of information I uncovered during my visit to Weiden, this was probably the most disturbing. The thought of Nazi officials doing their vile business in my grandfather's house, perhaps even sleeping in his bed, made my stomach twist. Had my father known this, I wondered, and if he did why hadn't he shared it with us?

Outside the station Inge gave me a gentle hug. She had learned

English by listening to jazz and other American popular music as a child, and she often sprinkled our conversation with colloquialisms and clichés. So I suppose I shouldn't have been surprised by her parting words as I climbed onto the train: "See you later, alligator."

During the three-hour train ride to Munich I tried to make sense of my five-day visit to Weiden. So much had happened in such a short period of time that my head was literally spinning. From the moment I stepped foot in my father's hometown I felt as if I had been swept into a whirlwind marked by a series of surprising discoveries and uncanny coincidences. Stumbling upon the offices of *Der Neue Tag* and meeting Inge. Being invited to attend the final gathering at the glass factory the Kupfers had once owned and talking to workers who remembered Dad and his father. Meeting Eddie Wittmann and his father Karl, a former business associate of my grandfather's. Visiting Frankenreuth, the site of the Kupfers' first foundry, and talking to Adam Dobner. Finding the family gravesite in Weiden. And – most surprising of all – discovering that the Kupfer villa had been occupied by the Nazis and destroyed by the Americans.

At times it felt as if I had stepped onto the set of a movie in which I was scripted to play the leading role. Given the pace of developments, it was clear that I could spend another month in Weiden and find plenty to keep me occupied. But the expiration date of my monthlong Eurail Pass was ticking down and I was eager to continue my grand tour of Europe.

I wondered what my father would have made of it all. I hoped he would be proud of me for returning to his hometown and unearthing the remnants of his past. But perhaps he would be angry at me for visiting the place where his father and millions of other Jews had been cast aside and murdered, and for accepting the hospitality of people who had permitted, if not participated in, the genocide.

It was hard not to like the people I had met in Weiden. They were warm, welcoming and down to earth. I was invited into people's living rooms and kitchens, without fanfare or fuss, for coffee, cake, and conversation. Many people expressed regret for what had happened to my grandfather and the other Jewish residents, but this was often followed by the explanation, "We didn't know what was happening." I heard that phrase so often that it began to seem practiced, as if they had been taught to say it. All they knew, I was told, was that the Jewish families gradually disappeared, one by one, without notice or explanation. Some, like my father, who had money or political connections, were able to escape. Others were sent away, but no one knew exactly where. Yes, they had heard about the concentration camps, but they thought those were for dangerous criminals, Jews and Christians alike. No one admitted to knowing about gas chambers or mass shootings or the other Nazi atrocities.

Even Inge told me that when she was a little girl and asked her parents about the Holocaust, they said they were unaware of what was really happening. "I didn't know!" her mother told her. "We were told that the concentration camps were filled with murderers and other serious criminals."

One elderly woman I met recounted an episode that occurred toward the end of the war. She and her mother were out shopping when a work crew from a nearby camp – most likely this was Flossenbürg – were herded through town. The prisoners were in bad shape, the woman recalled, and when she went over to talk to one of them a guard shooed her away, warning her that the men were dangerous criminals.

Another woman recalled that the first sign of trouble was the appearance of large trunks in front of the homes of Jewish families. The Jews and their belongings were taken to the railroad station and loaded onto a train, and that was the last anyone heard of them. Their houses were seized by the government and sold. What happened to the evicted Jews, I asked? Apparently, no one knew or bothered to find out.

Many people told me that the Jews and Gentiles in Weiden had a good relationship until Hitler came to power. Everyone got along and respected each other. It was only the Nazis who stirred up trouble and fostered hatred of the Jews. But this conveniently overlooked the long history of antisemitism in Bavaria, including the establishment of antisemitic societies in Weiden[7] and other cities decades before the rise of National Socialism.

I have no idea if any of the people I spoke to had been Nazis or were complicit in any way in the Holocaust. Some no doubt knew more than they were letting on, but for many others, perhaps their only sin was looking the other way – a sin millions of other Germans were guilty of as well.

I also heard about individual acts of courage. Eduard Wittmann's grandfather Josef had allowed a Polish Jew to hide in his factory and Johann Herold, the gas station attendant I met in Frankenreuth, told me he was arrested after he helped to sell the property of a Jewish friend who had fled to London.

I must admit I enjoyed being the center of attention during my visit to Weiden, but I never felt completely at ease. I couldn't help wondering whether the people I met were genuinely interested in me and my quest to learn about my father's family or were acting out of a sense of collective – or personal – guilt over what had happened to their Jewish neighbors.

Those reservations did not apply to Eddie, who tragically died in a car accident many years ago, nor to Inge, who remains a friend to this day. I did sometimes wonder why Inge had been so quick to take me under her wing and champion my cause. I assumed it was simply because she was a good person who felt drawn to help a clueless young American. While that was probably true, she recently shared a story that revealed a deeper motive.

During the war her parents had lived next door to a Jewish couple in the nearby town of Amberg. The couple had always been very kind to her mother, spending many hours with her sharing their love of art and culture. "They were her teachers and the source of ideas for many later stages in her life," Inge told me. They even allowed her mother to hang her swimming suit in their laundry room so that Inge's grandfather, a strict disciplinarian who forbade his daughter from going swimming, wouldn't discover the wet suit.

One day the couple disappeared without a word. Her mother never saw them again. The tragedy that befell her Jewish neighbors "weighed on my mother until her last days," Inge recalled. One of her last wishes was for her daughter to "please say how sorry I am about what happened during the Nazi years."

Adam Dobner and me in Frankenreuth, 1979

PART II

STARTING OVER

On October 15, 1937, my father crossed the border from Kehl, in the southwest corner of Germany, into Strasbourg, France. His German passport was stamped with a 15-day transit visa to attend l'Exposition Internationale in Paris, an event devoted to "art and technology in modern life." The exposition, which featured pavilions from 44 countries, including a menacing German tower crowned by an eagle and swastika designed by Nazi architect Albert Speer, attracted more than 31 million visitors, but whether Dad was among them is not clear. Nor do I know whether he met his older brother Ernst, who had immigrated to France four years earlier.

Five days after entering France, Dad boarded the SS *Bremen* in Cherbourg for the five-day voyage across the Atlantic to New York. The *Bremen*, the jewel of the Norddeutscher Lloyd fleet, had set out from her home port of Bremerhaven on October 19 and called on Southampton before arriving in Cherbourg. The sleek, bulbous-bowed ship was carrying more than 2,000 passengers, many of whom, like my father, were fleeing Nazi Germany.[1]

Although German shipping lines had an express policy of downplaying Nazism, the *Bremen*'s crew included a Nazi Party cell and a unit of the SA, Hitler's brown-shirted storm troopers.[2] The ship had often been the target of anti-Nazi demonstrations while docked in New York, including one in July 1935, when protesters stormed the luxury liner and tore down the swastika flag fluttering from the jackstaff and tossed it into the Hudson.[3]

The *Bremen* steamed into New York Harbor on Monday, October 25, slipping past the outstretched torch of the Statue of Liberty on her port side and tacking toward the phalanx of skyscrapers ringing Lower Manhattan. As she made her way up the Hudson and slowly swung into Pier 86 in Midtown, the needle-nosed spire of the Empire State Building and, beyond that, the terraced crown of the Chrysler Building shimmered in the distance.

When he stepped off the gangway at the Hudson River piers Dad was greeted by his sponsor, Siegfried Herrmann, an elderly uncle of his mother through marriage. The youngest of eight children, Herrmann was 16 when he immigrated to the United States in 1882, long before my father was born, so it's unlikely the two men had ever met before. Dad had a few other distant relatives and family friends scattered around the New York metropolitan area, but other than that he was the proverbial stranger in a strange land.

He brought with him a trunk packed with an assortment of fine clothes: bespoke suits; monogrammed silk shirts; Italian leather shoes, riding breeches, and boots; silk ties, handkerchiefs, and ascots. It also contained a red leather album, thick as the Manhattan telephone directory, containing his stamp collection; an Underwood portable typewriter[4]; a pocket-sized Zeiss Ikon folding camera (which today sits on the bookcase in my living room) and a pair of Zeiss binoculars in a battered brown leather case; a diamond encrusted stick pin that had belonged to his father as well as a few other modest pieces of jewelry; and a violin in a velvet-lined case from his schoolboy days.

Tucked in his coat pocket was another item that would play a pivotal role in establishing his new life in America: a custom-made platinum cigarette case. There were draconian restrictions on the amount of money and other valuables Jewish emigrants could take out of Germany at the time. They were allowed to carry no more than 10 reichsmarks, or about $4, in cash, and there were further limits on the amount of funds they could transfer abroad from German banks.

They were also required to pay an onerous emigration tax, called *Reichsfluchtsteuer*. These measures, designed to drain Jews of their assets, had their intended effect: the vast majority of German Jewish refugees arrived in their new countries essentially as paupers.[5]

The cigarette case had been made for the express purpose of circumventing those restrictions. Platinum is exponentially more valuable than silver – in 1937 it was worth $47 an ounce, compared to 45 cents an ounce for silver – but to the unschooled eye it can pass for its more quotidian cousin. Dad later sold the case for more than $2,000, a princely sum in those days.

But the most cherished item of all, at least to me, was a photo album containing snapshots of family, friends, and landscapes. The slender, canvas-covered volume was organized by location and date neatly written in white ink on its taupe-colored pages, with the pictures themselves sometimes annotated in black ink. Dad is usually pictured in the company of family and friends, and more often than not there is an attractive, well-turned-out young woman hanging on his arm.

One woman in particular was a frequent companion. Her name was Lotte Roderer, and with her round, open face, engaging smile, sparkling eyes, and wavy dark hair she bore a striking resemblance to Ingrid Bergman. It's clear from the pictures that Dad and Lotte were close friends, most likely lovers. There are pictures of them dressed to the nines standing in front of a palatial hotel in Karlsbad,[6] the fashionable Czech spa town, strolling in a wooded park, posing arm-in-arm and ski-to-ski in the Alps. Perhaps the most telling picture shows Lotte lying languorously with her eyes closed on a bench next to my grandfather, looking perfectly at ease, as if she were a member of the family.

Aunt Nan, my mother's older sister, once mentioned that she knew a "big secret" about my father, but she wouldn't say what it was. I can't help wondering if the secret was that Dad had been engaged to Lotte or another woman before he left Germany. It seems unlikely that he had been married because, in one of Otto's letters to his son after he immigrated to America, my grandfather impatiently asks when he would announce an engagement. Then again, it would almost be more surprising if Dad hadn't been married before he came to the States. After all, he was a handsome, urbane young man from an affluent Jewish family. And it's apparent from the photographs that he was popular with the ladies. That impression was confirmed by Christina Gottshall, the elderly woman I met during my first visit to Weiden.

Dad settled in New Haven, where Sig Herrmann owned a successful tailoring business. He lived with Herrmann and his family until he got a job and could support himself. His first job was working as a night clerk at a residential hotel in a sketchy neighborhood near the railroad station. He earned $10 a week, which even in those days was a paltry sum.[7]

In January 1939, he took a job as a door-to-door salesman for the J.R. Watkins Company, a Minnesota-based maker of soaps, spices, and other household products.[8] He apparently did well. Within a few months he was earning three times as much as he had at the hotel, and within a year he was promoted to district sales manager, responsible for managing a team of 15 salesmen in southwest Connecticut. In January 1941, he moved 20 miles down the coast to Bridgeport, where Watkins' district office was located.

In October of that year, Eastern Division Sales Manager A.F. Newman sent Dad a letter praising him for the success of his sales team in a liniment promotion: "Of all the reports coming in over this desk on Monday morning, none gave us any bigger kick than the one coming from Bridgeport with a total sales of $314.20, and 245 Liniment Combinations. Congratulations!" he wrote. "Seventeen dealers qualified for the free Petro-Carbo Salve in the first week, and this is really something!" A few weeks later Newman sent his southwest Connecticut manager another letter commending him for setting a sales record for the district: "$357.14 sets up a new all-time record at Bridgeport and we certainly want to take this opportunity to say, 'Congratulations on a fine job.'"

Dad ended his relationship with Watkins in February 1942, after three years with the company. The reason, according to a letter he sent to the US Attorney in Hartford seeking permission to travel,[9] was that he had been inducted into the Army. Among Dad's papers I found several letters from the Selective Service ordering him to report for induction on various dates, but he never spoke about serving in the Army or any other branch of the military, and I found no evidence that he ever did.[10] It's possible he was rejected because of his status as an enemy alien, but that seems unlikely because tens of thousands of German-born Jews served in the US military during the war, including his cousin Erich.[11] More likely it was for medical reasons – he had a long history of back problems, which was why he always slept with a sheet of plywood under his mattress.

In any event, he took a job later that year as a machine operator at a Bridgeport company that made tools, spare parts, and other equipment for the military. He also attended a night class based on Dale Carnegie's best-selling book, *How to Win Friends and Influence People*. The social primer was all the rage at the time. It was even popular in Nazi Germany.

Dad with Lotte Roderer, Karlsbad, circa 1935

GETTING OUT

Dad's business success came despite being preoccupied by something far weightier than liniment promotions – trying to get his father out of Germany. The correspondence I found in my parents' attic chronicled the growing concern both men felt as they encountered one obstacle after another. Otto tried to put on a brave face, but his frustration and worry become more evident as time passed and conditions deteriorated.

They received conflicting information about the proper procedures to follow to obtain a visa and secure a precious berth on a transatlantic ship. There was also confusion about who had jurisdiction over what and which routes offered the best chance of success. Some said you needed a US visa before you could book passage on a ship. Others said, no, you must secure a berth before the American Consulate would issue a visa. The best hope was on an American-flagged ship, or a Spanish – or Portuguese – one. It was better to embark from Lisbon, or Bilbao, or perhaps Vigo – and sail to Havana, or Santo Domingo, or maybe Buenos Aires. One should book passage through the American Joint Distribution Committee (JDC) or another aid organization. Or was it better to book directly with a shipping line?

Dad and Otto pursued several of these scenarios, but their efforts always ended in disappointment. As I read through their correspondence, I couldn't help but feel angry. Anger at the Nazis, of course, but also at the US government and the aid agencies that made it so difficult for my grandfather and other Jews to get out of Germany.

The situation was taking a toll on Dad as well. In a letter to his cousin Lisl in England, in March 1941, he wrote: "At the moment I am rather down with my nerves and am constantly losing weight, which I apparently cannot stop despite medical treatment." He complained that he had had only eight days of vacation since arriving in the US, a period of more than three years, "and even they were spoiled by bad weather."

The correspondence reveals how heartbreakingly close Dad came to saving his father. On April 14, he wrote Otto that he had submitted an affidavit to the US Consul in Stuttgart in support of his visa application. He had also sent funds to the JDC to cover the cost of a berth on a ship from Lisbon to the US as well as rail travel from the German frontier to Lisbon. "… so the only thing you need to do is to book the sea passage as soon as it is available," he assured his father. But three weeks later, after spending a long day in New York visiting the offices of one transatlantic shipping company after another, he concluded that "nowhere in America with any line is even a single shipping berth to be had."

According to documents I obtained from the Hessen State Archives in Germany, Otto had been granted a visa to immigrate to the UK in 1939 (Mina's daughter, Rosl Klein, lived in London), but for some reason he never used it. Among the personal effects he declared to the German government at the time was a cigarette case, which may well have been a replica of the custom-made platinum case Dad brought with him when he immigrated to the US.[1]

Not only did Dad have to contend with a volatile political situation in Europe and variable immigration policies and procedures, but he also had to deal with apparent apathy by members of his own family. Siegfried's son Albert, a lawyer in New Haven, had agreed to make an affidavit in support of Otto's application for a US visa, but apparently he was taking his time in doing so. In a letter to Albert on April 8, 1940, Dad vented his frustration:

Dear Albert,

Our short telephone conversation of last Saturday was a terrific shock to me. As you know I am waiting for this affidavit for nearly a half a year now. After you gave me the last time in December definite assurances that you will make it out in the shortest possible time, I naturally was relying completely on this promise and let valuable time pass by, without contacting any other people. This problem has now reached a stage where no time can be lost any longer unless I should decide to let my father starve to death. In the meantime I had the most difficult task in giving my father all kind of excuses in reply to every single letter of increasing desperation on that subject; to a man whose only hope in life is pinned upon this piece of paper, meaning to him protection against deportation to the Lublin area,[2] finally getting away from Germany and being together with me again.

Dad assured Albert that neither he nor Otto would be a burden on him or his father. He pointed out that both he and Fritz Klein, another relative on his mother's side of the family, were sponsored by Siegfried when they immigrated to the US, and neither had turned to the Herrmanns for financial support.

He [Siegfried] can be absolutely assured that those people for whom he guaranteed never will give him any trouble whatsoever. ... Fritz has a very rich brother-in-law in Buenos Aires, with whom he is on best terms and who proposes in every letter full financial support if necessary. The other fellow's name is Robert Kupfer whom you know well enough, I am afraid.

Noting that Siegfried "is an old gentleman" whose guarantee may not be "sufficiently recognized by the American Consul," Dad urged

Albert to take the initiative. "I would much rather have you make out this affidavit because the least I can afford at this already critical moment is a further delay caused by possible technical mistakes. If you would comply with my desire, which I desperately hope, I shall back up the already given verbal assurances by the following offer to you." He then listed five inducements: 1) $5,000 cash, 2) the platinum cigarette case he brought from Germany, which he valued at $1,700, 3) his stamp collection, worth an estimated $1,500, 4) a promise to submit his own affidavit on behalf of his father, pledging full financial support, and 5) a statement from J.R. Watkins verifying that Dad was earning an average of $30 a week.

The affidavit "is nothing but a pure formality without the slightest consequence for the signer," Dad assured his cousin. "I have put all my cards on the table and cannot do more. I wish you would do me this one favor before it is too late and I would be grateful to you all my life." He concluded by saying he would like to come to New Haven "to hear your final decision," adding "I am inviting myself for supper, if you don't mind, I think you know that I am very fond of a good meal."

Despite his entreaties, it appears that Albert continued to drag his feet. On February 8, 1941, 10 months after the previous letter, Dad wrote Albert that he just received a letter from his father stating that his visa number finally has been called by the American Consul and he has been asked to submit an affidavit as soon as possible: "You can imagine how glad I am to know that my father has a good chance now to get away from it all and escape the always threatening possibility to be sent to one of these camps, which one has a good right to say amounts to as much as saving somebody's life."

But for reasons the correspondence does not make clear, Otto apparently never received the visa.

After being repeatedly thwarted in their efforts to have Otto immigrate to the US, Dad and his father turned their focus elsewhere. In November 1941, Otto was granted a visa to enter Cuba and Dad booked him a berth on a steamer sailing from Vigo to Havana. The ship was scheduled to depart on December 15, but delays in obtaining the required documents and arranging transit to Spain foiled the plan.

Nearly a year later, on October 1, 1942, Otto was granted a second visa to enter Cuba. But by then it was too late. He and Mina had been deported to Theresienstadt on August 18.

Theresienstadt

STORMY WEDDING

Despite his modest beginnings in the United States, with little money and few contacts, Dad apparently wasted little time climbing the Jewish social ladder in Connecticut. In a letter to Albert in February 1941, he wrote, "I have been frequently invited to Judge Shapiro's and I have always had a good time there." He was no doubt referring to Louis Shapiro, a judge who lived in the affluent Hartford suburb of Farmington. Shapiro was later elected to the state House of Representatives and went on to become the chief judge of the state Superior Court and an associate justice of the state Supreme Court.

In the same letter Dad also mentioned that he had met a prominent Jewish attorney named Sam Friedman and had been invited to Friedman's house in Southport, a tony Fairfield County suburb. At the time of their meeting, Friedman was working as a defense counsel in one of the most sensational criminal cases of the day. It involved Joseph Spell, a Black chauffeur accused of raping a wealthy Greenwich socialite and throwing her off a bridge, an incident trumpeted in newspaper headlines as a "lurid orgy" and "night of horror."[1] Friedman's co-counsel was none other than Thurgood Marshall, then the NAACP's top lawyer. Spell was eventually acquitted and Marshall, of course, went on to become the first African-American justice on the Supreme Court.[2]

Dad once mentioned to my cousin Jean Adnopoz, who lives in a Tudor-style mansion in Hamden, a northern suburb of New Haven, that he was familiar with the house because he had known the previous occupants. The former owners were William Brewster, a scion of one of the wealthiest and most prominent families in New Haven, and his wife, Phebe.[3] Jean had no clue how Dad knew the Brewsters or what their relationship might have been, but if he had been a guest in their home he was evidently traveling in some fancy social circles.

Dad's bachelor days came to an end when he met Gertrude Schwartz, a tall, dark-haired beauty who bore more than a passing resemblance to Joan Crawford. Gert, who was a friend of Albert Herrmann's sister Bertha, lived with her parents a few blocks from the Herrmanns in the East Rock neighborhood of New Haven.[4]

Like my father, my mother's parents, Samuel and Sara Schwartz, had immigrated to the United States to escape religious persecution. They arrived in 1904, fleeing Jewish pogroms in Ukraine, which was then part of the Russian Empire. They came from Rzhyshchiv, a small city on the Dnieper River southeast of Kyiv, where Sam had been the captain of a riverboat that carried grain down to the Black Sea.[5]

In 1996, during a three-week trip to Russia and Ukraine, I made an excursion to Rzhyshchiv. Nearly a century had passed since my grandparents lived there, so I had little hope of finding any remnants of their past, but I was curious to see where they had come from. The city is only about 40 miles from Kyiv, but the bus ride over narrow, bumpy roads seemed to take forever. I arrived in early afternoon to find a town that looked like a scene out of *Fiddler on the Roof*. Rutted dirt roads lined with ramshackle wood houses languished behind rickety picket fences. The place seemed deserted except for a few children skipping through puddles and chickens strutting and clucking in the yards.

The few people I came across looked at me as if I had dropped out of the sky. I tried to communicate, but given that I didn't speak a word of Ukrainian or Russian and none of the people I approached spoke more than a few words of English, my efforts were almost comical in their futility. I did manage to learn that most of the city's records had been destroyed – either in a flood or a fire, I don't remember which – dashing my hopes of finding any official documents about my mother's family.[6]

Sam and Sara settled in Stamford, on the Connecticut side of Long Island Sound, 40 miles northeast of New York City. A few years later they moved to Hartford, where they lived briefly before putting down roots in New Haven. They had four children, born about four years apart. The eldest, Abraham, or Abe, was born in Rzhyshchiv in 1903 and was an infant when his parents emigrated. Next came Hannah, whom everyone called Nan, and then Max – Mac to family and close friends – both of whom were born in Stamford. My mother, the baby of the family, was born in 1915 in New Haven.[7]

Sam founded a small company called The Connecticut Waist & Dress Co., which manufactured ladies' dresses and blouses. The business must have done reasonably well because in 1919 he purchased a three-family house on Willow Street, two blocks from East Rock Park, for $6,500.

The family's fortunes took a dark turn when Abe contracted meningitis, an infection of the membranes covering the spinal cord and brain, a condition that left him bedridden much of the time and forced him to use crutches or a wheelchair to get around. He was only 19 when he died in 1922.

Abe's long illness and death had a profound impact on the family. My grandmother forbade her surviving children from playing music in the house for a year. She hung a portrait of her first-born above her bed, where it remained until her death nearly 40 years later. Abe's crutches, books, and other personal effects were tucked away in a locked hallway closet – Sara's secret shrine to her elder son. Survivors' guilt, common among Holocaust survivors like my father, was apparently instilled in my mother's side of the family as well.

My parents were both Ashkenazi Jews who grew up in not particularly religious homes, but that's pretty much where the similarities ended. Dad was the son of a wealthy industrialist who grew up in a world of big houses, fancy cars, and vacations at fashionable resorts. Although he had a limited education, attending business school rather than university, he was worldly and well-traveled. Now, in America, he found himself a lonely refugee approaching middle age. His parents were both dead, his only sibling, his older brother Ernst, lived an ocean apart in France, and his closest relative in the US, his cousin Erich, lived several hours away in a small town in Upstate New York.

My mother, on the other hand, grew up in a tight-knit family of modest means. Although both Nan and Mac went to college,[8] Mom graduated high school in 1932, in the midst of the Great Depression, and Sam didn't have enough money for her to follow suit. She attended secretarial school instead and worked in a series of clerical positions. She was 31, eight years younger than Dad, and had lived with her parents in the same house virtually her entire life. With the exception of a road trip to Ohio to visit relatives, she had never traveled beyond the Northeast.

I'm not sure how long or what form my parents' courtship took, but knowing Dad, who had a romantic streak and enjoyed dining out, there were probably quite a few dinners at candlelit restaurants, and knowing Mom, a devout homebody, there were likely a fair share of quiet meals at home with her parents.

They were married in September 1946 at Aunt Nan and Uncle Ab's (short for Abner) stately brick colonial in Hamden. My parents were not society people by any means, but an article about their wedding appeared in the *New Haven Register* – most likely because the Society editor was a family friend. The ceremony was performed "in a white floral setting" with a program of violin, piano, and cello music, the *Register* reported. Mom wore "a champagne nylon satin gown and a matching tulle halo trimmed with ostrich tips."

Shortly before the afternoon ceremony was to begin, the skies turned ominously dark and unleashed a torrential rain. Half a century later, in a memory book I put together for Mom's 80th birthday, the downpour still lingered in the minds of the guests. "As the evening hour of the ceremony neared, the skies began to lower," recalled Uncle Mac's wife, Roz. "Clouds for miles around emptied oceans of water."

Roz's appraisal of her new brother-in-law was a favorable one: "Robert was a sweet man who obviously would be an admirable companion through life." As the newlyweds set off on their honeymoon, she remembered, "Robert smiled ... and Gert masked what she was feeling, but as I play the film of their years together, I see quiet pleasure and contentment with each other. Robert's pleasure in his boys was always evident."

The newlyweds had planned a monthlong honeymoon, driving down to Miami Beach by way of Savannah and then sailing to Havana on a cruise ship. In the wake of World War II, the Cuban capital had become a popular destination for American tourists because of its tropical beauty and lively – some might say licentious – nightlife.[9] But my parents never got to experience Cuba's allures. On October 6 a hurricane ripped across the island, leaving five people dead and disrupting ship traffic in the Florida Straits.

After their abridged honeymoon, Dad joined his father-in-law's business making women's blouses. Compared with the large, far-flung glassmaking business his family had run in Germany, Sam Schwartz's operation must have seemed like small potatoes, but it was a step up from his previous jobs as a hotel desk clerk, door-to-door salesman, and machinist. Five years later, after Sam died, he took over the business.

My brother Richard was born two days before Christmas 1949, and I came along 19 months later, in July 1951. Considering my parents married relatively late – Dad was 39 and Mom 31 – it's surprising they waited more than three years to have kids, but I suspect money was a factor.

Mom and Dad on Wedding Day, September 1946

MATRIARCHY

Dad married into a family of powerful, strong-willed women. My grandmother was a stern, no-nonsense matriarch who didn't suffer fools gladly. "She was tough as nails. Dominant," recalled Nan's daughter, Jean, who grew up in the first-floor flat of her grandparents' house – the same apartment I grew up in 20 years later.

Sara was a stout woman with a round face framed by short, white hair and thick, slightly bowed legs that appeared to connect to her feet without the benefit of ankles. Her swollen appendages were symptomatic of "milk leg," a painful condition associated with childbirth.[1] She wore thick rubber stockings for support, but even so she was prone to falling.

Nana might have been a tough cookie, but she had a soft spot for her youngest grandson. In her eyes I was the perfect little prince who could do no wrong, and I in turn adored her. She was my best friend, my champion and protector. Her second-floor flat was my safe space, a demilitarized zone that not even my mother dared violate. Whenever I got into hot water with Mom, a not infrequent occurrence, I would race up the back steps into Nana's ample, welcoming arms.

Nana was a good cook and our flat was often filled with the enticing aromas of borscht, kugel, fresh-baked challah, and other

Jewish dishes wafting down from her kitchen. I was anointed her official taster, prefiguring my own interest in cooking. One of my favorite snacks was gribenes, the greasy, crispy scraps of chicken skin and onion left over from making schmaltz. I could devour a whole bowl of grievies, as I called them, in a few minutes, which invariably left me grieving with a nasty stomachache.

Like her mother, Aunt Nan was a formidable woman who commanded attention. She was short, a full head closer to the ground than Mom, but what she lacked in physical stature she more than made up for with her glamorous looks and dynamic personality. Unlike my mother, who tended to be reserved in unfamiliar social settings – a reticence she more than compensated for around her immediate family – Nan was naturally social. She had lots of friends and was always dashing around to card games, luncheons, and dinner parties. I can still picture her roaring up our driveway in her hulking Chrysler New Yorker, her snowy hair barely visible above the steering wheel, charging up the back steps and bursting into our kitchen as if she owned the place. *Helloooo. Anyone home?*

I always looked forward to having dinner at Nan and Ab's house. Compared to our modest two-bedroom ranch-style house, their spacious colonial, set back on a large corner lot, seemed like Downton Abbey. There were lots of rooms to explore and even a narrow "secret staircase" in the rear that led to the maid's quarters (though I don't recall them ever having a live-in maid).

Nan was a good cook, too, and she made a point of serving the best of everything in abundance. Hors d'oeuvres might consist of creamy chopped liver, mini kosher hot dogs with spicy mustard, warm cheese puffs, and chilled jumbo shrimp (yes, we were bad, *trayf*-eating Jews). The main course was often buttery beef tenderloin or roasted Cornish hens served with crisp latkes or noodle pudding. For dessert there was homemade pie or cake or, my favorite, an ethereal chocolate roll slathered with whipped cream.

My parents always cautioned Richard and me to be on our best behavior when we went to Nan and Ab's. They were especially concerned about my tendency to overindulge, a proclivity that prompted Richard to nickname me "the human vacuum cleaner."

Despite my skeletal appearance – I was little more than an assemblage of bones that, miraculously, managed to move – I was capable of consuming prodigious amounts of food. (I wasn't the most discriminating eater, either. Our next-door neighbor once brought over some leftover beef bones for our dog Lucky. Suffice it to say Lucky never got a lick.)

As we walked up the flagstone path to their front door, Dad would lean over and whisper, "Don't be a *fresser!*" employing the German term for glutton. But in the presence of all that glorious food, I tended to lose any semblance of self-control. I would pretend not to notice Dad glaring at me as I stuffed my face like a street urchin who hadn't had a decent meal in days. Would I care for a second (or third) slice of beef? Nan would inquire. Another helping of noodle pudding? A second piece of pie, perhaps? Oh, yes, yes, yes! You bet I would!

Nan was always a gracious host, but as I grew older I became increasingly aware that there was a certain divide between her family and ours. My parents were rarely included in the dinner conversation or asked for their opinion. What annoyed me most was the way Dad was treated. He wasn't as well educated or affluent as Nan's family, but he had endured hardships they could hardly imagine. I remember one evening when Dad was making a point – a rare event in itself – when he was cut off with not so much as an "excuse me." I felt like standing up and shouting: *Listen to him, dammit! Listen to what he has to say!* But I didn't. I just sat there, quietly chewing my tenderloin.

Aunt Roz was another force to be reckoned with. Although we saw her infrequently, she never failed to make an impression. A short woman with close-cropped gunmetal gray hair and a narrow, angular face, she taught psychology at Yale and was a co-founder of a community art school in New Haven. She was a smart, independent woman who flouted convention – the type of woman my mother and Nan, who valued tradition and family loyalty above all, could not abide.

Roz made no secret of her left-wing political views, which did not always play well at family gatherings. While my parents were diehard Democrats, other members of the clan were more conservative. I can still picture her jabbing the air with a lipstick-tipped cigarette wedged between her fingers as she denounced the latest injustice by the Nixon or Reagan administrations.

Although I was a bit intimidated by Roz's flinty personality, I found myself gravitating toward her at family gatherings. We often had lengthy conversations about our shared interests in art, politics, and travel. This never failed to annoy Mom, who suggested on more than one occasion that my aunt might not be a good influence on me.

I admired Roz and was flattered by her interest in me, but there was one incident during Dad's funeral that I never forgave her for. We had just gotten into a black town car after the service at the synagogue – Mom, Richard, and me in the back seat, Roz and Mac up front next to the driver – when she snapped open her purse, pulled out a cigarette, and lit up. It was a cool, gray late September afternoon and the windows were closed, trapping the smoke inside. I waited for Mac or someone else to say something, but there was only silence as we slowly made our way across town to the Jewish cemetery in Westville. I was a smoker myself, but I couldn't believe that Roz had the *chutzpah* to light up at such an inappropriate time. As the smoke wafted in my face, I felt a slick of rage spooling up from the pit of my stomach. I was tempted to wrap my hands around her neck and shake the cigarette out of her mouth, but I just sat there and fumed in silence.

My mother was a formidable woman in her own right. She reigned with unchallenged authority at home, but outside of her little fiefdom she wasn't as commanding or self-assured. As I got older I came to realize that she was a deeply insecure woman whose iron-fisted domestic rule was her way of compensating for feelings of inadequacy.

I always suspected Mom resented the fact that she never got the chance to go to college like Nan and Mac did, but whenever I broached the subject she promptly dismissed it. *Oh, don't be silly! That's just the way it was. Why would I resent my own sister and brother?* After secretarial school she went to work for her father and later became the executive secretary for a prominent local attorney.[2] She quit that job shortly before Richard was born and never worked outside the home again.

Even after she got married, Mom didn't venture far from the nest. She and Dad moved into the first-floor flat of her parents' house, just as Nan and Ab had before them. Every night after dinner she would dutifully trot upstairs to turn down the covers of her parents' bed and set out their slippers.

I sometimes wondered what it was like for my father to be surrounded by all these strong-willed, combative women. Between Nana, Aunt Nan, and Mom, there couldn't have been much oxygen left for a soft-spoken introvert. But I suspect part of him felt comforted and protected by the matriarchal order he lived under. After all, his own mother had died when he was 15, leaving him and his brother under the sway of an authoritarian father who was no doubt preoccupied with the demands of managing a large business.

With the Schwartz women running the show, there was no need for Dad to engage with the world beyond the requirements of his business. No need to voice his opinions or express his emotions. Even his social activities were tightly circumscribed; I never knew him to have a single friend of his own, independent of Mom and her circle.

Yet I imagine there were times when he felt profoundly alone, cut off as he was from everyone and everything he knew in the first 30 years of his life. Without those touchstones from the past did he ever feel alienated and adrift? Did he ever wake up in the middle of the night and wonder: *Where am I? Who is this demanding kvetch lying next to me and that hard-boiled babushka above us? And who are those foul-mouthed, unruly boys in the next room?*

Richard Dad and Me New Haven, circa 1955

Nana , Mom, Richard and Me, Willow St New Haven, circa 1956

WILLOW STREET

We lived in a neighborhood of stout, three-story shingled houses a mile or so from the neo-Gothic halls of Yale University. It was a tight-knit community of immigrant families, mostly Italian, Irish, and Jewish, the kind of place where everyone knew everyone else or acted as if they did. Two blocks away, College Woods, with its gnarled oaks, weedy playing fields, and cracked cement tennis courts, was our all-purpose playground.

Our backyard was a narrow rectangle of hard-packed dirt with a few patches of grass. Spring was announced each year by an exuberant azalea tree, which would burst into a glorious pink bouquet, like a peacock proudly displaying its plumage, providing a colorful backdrop for many family snapshots.

Old Mrs. Lutz lived next door in a dilapidated house overrun by feral cats. On Tuesday afternoon Pete the fishmonger came around in his battered green pickup, his glassy-eyed goods displayed on a bed of ice. The iceman would cometh once a week, lugging a block of ice up the back stairs and heaving it into Nana's icebox. On summer evenings the jingling bells of the Good Humor truck brought the neighborhood kids gleefully scurrying out of their houses.

Just about everyone I knew lived within a few blocks of our house. My best friend, Philip Greene, the soft-spoken, cerebral son of a Yale

English professor, lived around the corner. Richard and I had a friendly rivalry with our neighbors Frank and David Iaccarino, racing Go-Karts fashioned out of discarded orange crates and the chasses of old Radio Flyer wagons in summer and waging pitched battles with acorns in autumn and snowballs in winter.

I knew every alley and backyard in the neighborhood and felt safe wherever I went, but Mom wasn't so sanguine. She warned me to stay close to home and avoid the *shvartsa,* as she sometimes referred to Black people.[1] I didn't know exactly what the word meant, but I figured it wasn't intended as a compliment because it was usually uttered *sotto voce.* I was told in no uncertain terms to steer clear of Archie Moore's, a bar down the street frequented by Blacks and not infrequently the site of late-night altercations.

My parents were both loyal Democrats who nominally supported the civil rights movement, but they also betrayed a wariness of "colored people." In truth, they didn't trust anyone outside the *mishpucha,* especially anyone who wasn't a member of the Hebrew tribe. Given their backgrounds and the social climate of the time, their clannishness was probably not surprising or unusual, but it contributed to my own tendency to be distrustful of others.

Richard and I attended Worthington Hooker elementary school, a fortress-like brick building around the corner on Livingston Street. My first-grade teacher, a gray-haired spinster named Miss Deppensmith, taught me how to read – just as she had my mother 37 years earlier.

Two days before the 1960 election, Mom took Richard and me to a rally for John F. Kennedy at the New Haven Green. We were so far from the podium we could barely see the young senator from Massachusetts, but his distinctive voice, with those elegantly elongated A's amplified over scratchy speakers, held our attention. I still remember the thrill I felt two months later as we watched our dashing new president – coatless and hatless, his sandy hair fluttering in the frigid Washington air – take the oath of office as his glamorous wife looked on. For days afterward, Dad would recite passages from Kennedy's inaugural address, overlaying the president's silky Boston accent with his own guttural German one.

"Aaaask not what your country can do for you," he exhorted, pointing a finger at Richard and me, "aaaask what you can do for your country!" But it was the inaugural speech of another American president, Franklin Roosevelt, that provided the material for Dad's favorite political impression. "The only thing we have to fearrr," he would burr, his head quivering with gravitas, "is fearrr itself!"

Three years later, when an announcement came over the P.A. system at Sleeping Giant Junior High in Hamden that Kennedy had been shot, I rode the bus home in shocked silence. I huddled with Mom and Richard on the sofa in the den as we watched Walter Cronkite deliver the devastating news that the president was dead. When Dad got home that evening I could see tears glistening in the corner of his eyes. It was the closest I ever saw him come to crying.

After Nana died in 1960 and we moved to Hamden, a slumlord bought the house on Willow Street, chopped down the azalea, and paved over the backyard. It was my first lesson in the harsh realities of capitalism. How could someone destroy such a beautiful tree in the service of off-street parking?

As I survey the old neighborhood on Google Maps from a continent away in San Francisco, a warm, sad feeling washes over me. Even after all these years it still feels like home, still feels safe and comforting. The streets, shaded by oaks and maples and lined with the same sturdy wooden houses, look remarkably unchanged from half a century ago. Even our house looks the same, if a bit more forlorn. The stunted shrubs lining the front walk are somehow still clinging to life. The only unfamiliar note is a satellite dish attached to a pole in the front yard, gazing blankly at the street. And the paved-over backyard, where a car is parked on the spot where that wondrous azalea once stood.

BIG GERT AND LITTLE BOB

My parents were an odd couple in many respects. My mother was a buxom, big-boned woman with long arms and legs. Dad had a more delicate build with slender arms and legs and spindly wrists and ankles – Mom liked to call them "aristocratic." Although they were about the same height, five foot eight, Mom gave the appearance of being a lot bigger, especially when she was all *farpitzs*[1] with high heels and a lofty bouffant for an evening out.

That juxtaposition prompted one of my friends to dub them Big Gert and Little Bob. Of all the names Richard and I called our parents – and there were quite a few – those were the ones that really got under their skin. Whenever we tossed them out Mom's face would flush with anger and Dad would purse his lips and glare at us with wounded pride.

But it was their personalities more than their appearance that set them apart. When I think about my parents I picture my father in muted sepia tones and my mother in pulsing Kodachrome, practically jumping out of the frame. Dad tended to be cool, detached, and emotionally buttoned up; Mom was excitable, controlling, and constantly in your face. If his credo was "live and let live," hers was "*kvetch* and *kvetch* some more."

My mother found discord and dissatisfaction everywhere, and

where there was none she would manufacture it. The light was too bright or too dim, the volume too high or too low, the corned beef too fatty or too lean. Her sons were often the source of her discontent. Our hair was too long, our dress too sloppy, our language too vulgar, our music too shrill. As for Dad, his worst offense was that he wasn't around enough and when he was, he failed to adequately enforce the appropriate code of conduct for Richard and me.

I remember many nights being woken up by the sound of my mother's shrill voice piercing the wall between our bedrooms. *Bob, you've got to do something! They're getting away with murder!* The "they," of course, were Richard and me. Every now and then Mom's harangue would be interrupted by the low, reassuring rumble of Dad's voice. Then the rant would resume.

Despite their differences, or perhaps because of them, my parents had a powerful, unshakeable bond. Although they argued often – or should I say Mom argued and Dad listened – they never stayed mad at each other for long. Aside from Dad's occasional business trips or when he was in the hospital, they slept in the same bed every night of their married lives. They were a tight-knit team, and I never got the sense that there was much emotional distance between them.

My mother was a devoted wife, her commitment never more evident than after Dad was diagnosed with lymphoma in his early sixties. She was a tireless caregiver, feeding and washing him, making sure he took his myriad pills, and taking him to his endless doctors' appointments. Toward the end, when he was in the hospital for weeks at a time, she spent nearly every waking hour by his side, interrogating his doctors and riding herd over nurses and aides.

My father, in turn, adored my mother. Part of that adoration, I suspect, was simply gratitude that she and her family had taken him in. After all, he had come to this country with virtually no family or friends and few resources. The Schwartzes had provided him with a ready-made family, a close-knit clan of Eastern European Jews who shared his culture and values.

The letters and postcards Dad sent to Mom during his business trips reflect his deep affection for his wife as well as his playful sense of humor. Although English was not his native language, he wrote and spoke it with grace and wit. Even his handwriting, a tight, forward-tilting swirl, had a certain elegance.

"I am only one day gone and I am already lonely," he began one letter, in November 1958, written on stationery from the Wayside Motor Court in Danville, Virginia, where he and a colleague were staying while driving down to South Carolina. "The record shows that I have written to you already six postal cards! If this is not love?" He closed: "Love & Kisses Bob."

A few years later, in a letter written during another business trip down South, he began with a playful gambit: "Hi Baby. This is already the fifth day and hard to believe. How can you possibly endure such long separation? Are you positive you have only the girls over no male species?"

He had gone to see the movie *Irma la Douce* that evening "just to kill time." The next night he planned to take one of his salesmen and his wife to "a fancy supper club with dancing and a floor show," adding quickly, "I will not dance." He closed with a note of concern: "I hope you feel well and are not too lonely. Most of all I wish the kids would take care of you. I think they will I don't think they will let me down."

He never failed to bring his wife a gift when he returned from a business trip – a trinket for her charm bracelet, a new addition to her collection of wood and ceramic elephants, or perhaps a bottle of Chanel No. 5, her favorite fragrance. On special occasions, like her birthday, Mother's Day, and Christmas (we celebrated both Hanukkah and that other December holiday), he would present her with something more extravagant – a silk scarf, a jeweled brooch, an alligator-skin pocketbook. Sometimes he would give her a box of Russell Stover chocolates or a bouquet of sweetheart roses, her favorite flower, for no reason at all. He seemed to get as much pleasure out of giving the gifts as Mom did in receiving them.

The Hallmark cards that accompanied his offerings were usually of the sweet, syrupy variety, like the one that celebrates a woman's domestic talents, illustrated with cartoonish drawings of her merrily cooking, cleaning, mending clothes, and tending to her children's cuts and bruises – the kind of card that would be regarded today as hopelessly chauvinistic if not downright sexist.

One note, accompanying a Mother's Day gift (a compact, perhaps?) had a poetic touch:

I love the soft texture of your well-shaped face well enough and it is hard to visualize how this little gadget can further enhance an already existing beauty.

Yet here it is for you to use on Mother's Day.

For ever yours, Bob.

Just as he took pride in his own appearance, Dad took pleasure in his wife's as well. Mom was a smart dresser and Dad often complimented her on the way she looked. When she emerged from the bedroom dressed up for an evening out he would take a step back, look her up and down, and give a nod of approval. "What do you think, boys?" he would ask, turning to Richard and me. "Doesn't your mother look gorgeous?"

Their social circle consisted of a handful of Jewish couples who got together regularly for bridge, cocktail parties, dinners, and, as their children grew older, bar and bat mitzvahs, weddings, and other celebrations. Most of the men, like Dad, were in business, but there were also a lawyer or two, a doctor, and a journalist.[2] Typical of the era, most of the women were stay-at-home moms.

Although he tended to be a man of habit, Dad could be spontaneous at times. One evening he came home from work and, for no apparent reason, took Mom in his arms and waltzed her around the kitchen. "Oh, Bob, let me go! The brisket is burning!" she protested, as she tried to wiggle free, but Richard and I were delighted by the performance, whistling and applauding our approval.

DIFFERENT DAD

Dad wasn't like the other fathers I knew. For one thing, he was 44 when I was born, which was considerably older than most of my friends' fathers. Although he had an excellent command of English, he spoke with a thick German accent. Having grown up with that guttural elocution, I wasn't aware of how different it sounded until my friends started to make fun of him, mimicking him with an exaggerated growl.

He never took me camping or fishing or did other "guy stuff" that fathers typically do with their sons. He never helped me build a model airplane or work on a science fair project. On the rare occasions he tried to help me with my homework, it usually didn't go well, mainly because he had grown up with a very different educational system. When I once asked him to help me solve a simple mathematical equation, he proceeded to fill two sheets of paper with a blizzard of numbers, lines, and symbols that, as far as I was concerned, could have been Einstein's theory of relativity.

I savored the times I had Dad all to myself because they were rare. One of my earliest memories is going with him on a Saturday morning to his blouse factory on Crown Street in downtown New Haven. The narrow brick building was deserted on weekends, and while he packed orders I ran around among the rows of silent gray sewing machines and bolts of brightly colored fabric, my footsteps echoing on the wide wood-plank floors. When I got tired of exploring, I would crawl into an empty cardboard box and take a nap until he summoned me with the sharp two-toned whistle he deployed to call Richard and me (and, later, Lucky).

He generally used commissioned salesmen, but sometimes he made the rounds of local stores himself. Occasionally he let me tag along, provided I was neatly dressed and had pulled a comb through my hair. "This is my assistant salesman," he would tell the shopkeepers, most of whom were elderly Jewish men, which elicited a chuckle from them and a puffed-up chest from me.

On Sunday mornings Dad took charge of the kitchen to prepare brunch, and I was his eager sous chef. We walked – hand-in-hand, when I was young enough not to be embarrassed – down the hill to the neighborhood deli, where the air was perfumed with the sweet aroma of fresh-baked poppy seed and onion rolls piled in wire-mesh bins. Our shopping list usually consisted of German-style potato salad (made with oil instead of mayonnaise), pickled herring swimming in sour cream and onions, and – the one indispensable item as far as Dad was concerned – German sausage. His favorite was Weisswurst, a traditional Bavarian concoction made with veal, parsley, and cardamom, but he was also partial to Blutwurst, which, as the name suggests, is made with pig or cow's blood. I've always considered myself an adventurous eater, but I found those burgundy bangers utterly disgusting and refused to eat them. (Pickled pig's feet, another one of Dad's dubious culinary delights, also fell into that category.)

Another item he relished was Liederkranz, a soft, creamy cheese with a caustic aroma that could wake the dead or kill the living. Mom hated it because it would stink up her refrigerator for days, but I developed a taste for it. The cheese came wrapped in waxed paper inside a small wooden box, and Dad and I would happily polish off the whole container with half a loaf of Russian rye in a single sitting.

Dad and I were both introverts who were more comfortable communicating in writing than through the spoken word. Only a handful of the letters and cards we sent each other have survived, but I think they reveal a lot about our personalities and how we related to each other.

In October 1959, when I was eight and he was traveling down South on business, I wrote him a letter in a large, loopy script on wide-lined paper:

Dear pop,

I trust you are having a good time. I hope things are going good there. Things are going good at home. I hope I like my writing it is the best I can do. I suppose your business deal is coming along good. I am trying to write as much as I can. Today I was the teacher's pet and I had to go up and down stairs all day. We had Dinner at Aunt Nan last night and I bet you wish you were there. I hope you are having a good time now that I thing [sic] of it I hope the trip is not to long because we are missing you right at this very moment [turn over pop] if you want to know hows school its fin just fin. I hope your back in time for my money if you know what I mean. The family is getting tired not hering all your jokes.

A Deal of luck and kiss xxxxxxxxxx Pete

During the same trip he sent me a postcard from Whit's Motor Court in Newberry, South Carolina. I still remember the thrill I felt to receive a piece of mail addressed to me alone, especially from my father. The card contained only two sentences, but they filled a little boy's heart with joy and longing: "Dear Pete: Why is it that when I am away from you I miss you so? Have you been a good boy? Love, Daddy."

A couple of years later, when I was 10, I sent Dad a letter on stationery from the Riviera Congress Motor Inn on Tenth Avenue in New York, where the family had spent the night before he flew South on another business trip. "I hope you had a good plane trip there and that you are in good spirits," I wrote. "I had a lousy night as you must have noticed by the way I was twisting and turning." I suggested he write to us ("I THINK YOU KNOW THE ADRESS?") and closed with a warning: "Don't come home without a fortune." Richard added a brief postscript: "Bring firecrackers!" – a reference to the fact that South Carolina permitted the sale of more potent fireworks, like Roman candles and skyrockets, than Connecticut or New York did.

There were times when I longed for my father to be more like the other dads I knew, but I was also proud of his differences. Unlike many of my friends' fathers, who tended to be loud and loquacious, he was soft spoken and reserved. His courtly, old-world manner was particularly appealing to my mothers' female friends, who gravitated toward him at parties and other social events.

While other men tended to be careless or indifferent about their appearance, he was meticulous about his. On workdays he invariably wore a suit with a white handkerchief artfully tucked in his breast pocket, a freshly pressed button-down shirt, and a bowtie. His weekend attire usually consisted of a polo shirt, creased khakis, and buffed penny loafers. Although he died before T-shirts, jeans, and sneakers became the ubiquitous uniform for leisure activities, I can't even imagine him wearing such an outfit.

Dad rarely lost his temper, but when he did it was usually preceded by him muttering under his breath in German. I didn't understand what he was saying, but you didn't have to be bilingual to know he was pissed off. One afternoon, after Richard and I had locked our babysitter in the closet, he chased us down the alley next to our house, waving his leather belt and jabbering in his native tongue. I was scared shitless, but by the time he caught up with us he was too winded to inflict any serious damage.

I can count on one hand the number of times he actually hit me, and when he did, the punishment usually consisted of a few half-hearted *patsh aoyf di tokhes*[1] with a rolled-up newspaper. The so-called spanking was never very convincing. It was more about appeasing my mother than disciplining us. Dad, Richard, and I had an unspoken pact: put on a good show so Mom will believe we got religion.

The one thing that never failed to set him off was when he spilled something on his shirt during a meal. When that happened – God forbid! – he would whip the handkerchief out of his breast pocket, dip it into his water glass, and furiously dab at the offending spot while spewing Teutonic curses. Mom, Richard, and I would look on with morbid curiosity. If he successfully expunged the spot, we would resume eating as if nothing had happened; if not, a pall would hang over the rest of the meal.

Dad's company, Crown Shirts, specialized in making inexpensive knockoffs of ladies' designer blouses. We were not wealthy by any means – certainly nothing like the affluence he enjoyed in Germany – but we lived a comfortable middle-class life and Richard and I never wanted for anything.

As the owner of a small business, he worked long hours, which often included weekends. In the years when he commuted to New York, he usually left the house by 7 or 7:30 a.m. and didn't get home until nearly seven at night – and that's if the New York, New Haven & Hartford Railroad was running on time, which it usually wasn't.

By the time he got home he was tired and hungry and in no mood to deal with a pair of obstreperous boys and a battle-weary wife. Dinner conversation usually consisted of a mix of school news, current events, and local gossip, spiced with jokes Dad had heard at the office. The latter were usually of the "a rabbi and a priest were sitting at a bar" variety, but occasionally he cracked an off-color gag that would have Richard and me cackling with glee and Mom shaking her head reprovingly. "Oh Bob, not in front of the *kinder*," she would protest, as she tried to muffle her own laughter.

Saturdays were usually spent catching up on paperwork, but Sundays were generally devoted to relaxation and family time. Dad's favorite recreational activity was lounging on a chaise in the backyard, a newspaper in one hand and a good cigar in the other. That sedentary lifestyle became increasingly evident as he got older and his once trim waistline swelled.

During the summer Mom, Richard, and I spent almost every day at the Colony Beach Club, a predominantly Jewish swimming and racket club on the Sound in East Haven. Dad occasionally joined us after work for a late afternoon swim and a game of shuffleboard or ping-pong. I loved horsing around with him in the water, pressing my face against the mat of thick dark hair on his chest and breathing in his musky scent. We would swim out to the wooden raft anchored offshore and stretch out on the rough, sunbaked boards, basking in the briny tang of the ocean air as we watched the sun sink behind the distant smudge of Long Island.

Dad didn't have much interest in American popular culture, but he liked to watch TV. Ironically, one of his favorite programs was *Hogan's Heroes*, a '60s sitcom about American soldiers held in a German POW camp. I'm not sure if it was the German characters' bumbling incompetence or their over-the-top accents, but they always cracked him up.

Dad was a huge dog lover, a trait his younger son inherited. He was constitutionally incapable of walking past a dog without stopping to pet it. One of my favorite photographs from his German album shows him as a young boy, perhaps five or six, dressed in a sailor outfit and cradling a dachshund in his arms. Another photo, taken when he was in his twenties, shows him dressed in a suit and tie posing with what looks to be a schnauzer. The dog's name, curiously, was Peter.

From the time I was a small boy I pestered my parents to get me a dog. My persistence finally paid off on my 13th birthday. As I sat down for breakfast, I heard a whimpering sound coming from under the kitchen table. When I ducked down I saw a large ball of yellow fur quivering in a cardboard box lined with newspaper. I yelped with joy.

We dubbed him Lucky *Dreizehn* [Lucky 13]. Although he was officially my dog, it was clear from the beginning that Lucky's favorite human was my father. As soon as he heard Dad's car pull into the garage in the evening, he would start barking and running in circles around the kitchen. When the door opened he would launch himself at my father like a cougar, lapping at his face and nearly knocking him back down the steps.

The day I got Lucky was one of the happiest days of my life, and the day I found out he had died was one of the saddest. I was a sophomore at the University of Wisconsin and Dad had flown into Madison for a quick visit after a business trip to Chicago. We were eating dinner at a fancy restaurant on Lake Mendota when he broke the news. I tried not to cry but tears welled up under my eyelids. The duck a l'orange I had been savoring suddenly tasted like sandpaper.

Dad and Me New Haven, circa 1958

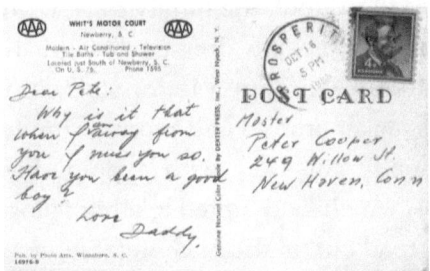

Postcard From Dad, 6 October 1959

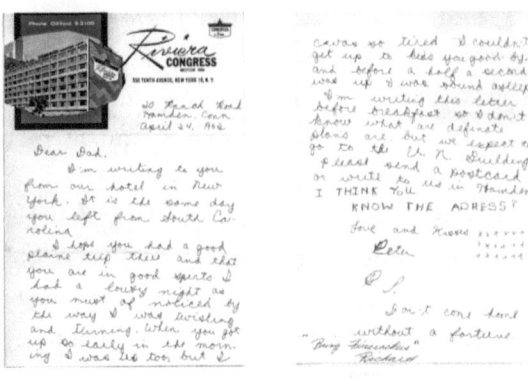

Letter to Dad, 1962

MATINEE

Once or twice a year Dad took the family to New York for a weekend matinee. In those days people dressed for the theater, especially people like my parents, who put a lot of stock in their appearance. Dad wore a sports jacket and tie and mom a simple dress and heels. Richard and I usually got away with a polo shirt, neatly pressed slacks, and oxfords, which Dad buffed to a high gloss the night before over newspaper spread out on the kitchen table.

We took the Merritt Parkway, a scenic highway that winds beneath a thick canopy of oak, maple, and birch and traverses a series of rivers, ponds, and tidal marshes. Driving on the Merritt felt like entering a magical kingdom, especially in autumn, when the trees burst into a dazzling bouquet of red, yellow, and orange leaves, and in winter, when the snow-shrouded branches transformed the narrow highway into a ghostly corridor.

As we approached New York the landscape grew darker and grittier. Neat suburban houses gave way to rusted bridges and water tanks, brick tenements scarred with graffiti, and empty lots littered with dismembered cars and abandoned appliances. The people changed too. Pink and white faces were replaced by brown and black ones. They sat on fire escapes and stoops, smoking cigarettes and drinking out of brown paper bags or peering out from behind barred windows. Even from the comfort of our blue Impala, the harshness and scarcity of their lives was palpable. For a cosseted middle-class boy from the pale white suburbs, these scenes were both fascinating and a little frightening.

Sometimes Dad would take us to lunch at the Horn & Hardart automat on Broadway, where the dishes were displayed in a wall of glass compartments. After several minutes of careful deliberation, I would drop some coins into a slot, slide open the door, and grab my prize. A few moments later the identical item would magically reappear, restocked by a worker hidden behind the wall. If we were short on time (and we usually were), we would grab some hot dogs and knishes from a street vendor in Times Square and wolf them down as we gazed bug-eyed at the giant billboards towering above us. I was particularly taken by the rugged-looking Winston man blowing puffs of real smoke from under his mustache.

Then Dad would take us by the hand and march us to the theater, dodging gawking sightseers and barking street vendors. My head swiveled left and right as we passed big-haired hookers in high heels and miniskirts preening in the shadows and muscular stagehands in tight T-shirts and rolled-up jeans smoking outside stage doors.

The first show I remember seeing was *The Music Man*, starring Bert Parks. I was giddy with anticipation as Dad led us through the throng milling outside the theater and into the gilded lobby. The red-velvet seats were frayed and lumpy, but that didn't dampen my excitement. As the lights faded and the curtain rose, we were magically transported from Midtown Manhattan to a small Midwestern town. I tapped my toes and bounced in my seat as Parks flashed his 1,000-watt smile and strutted across the stage as the band of boys blew their horns.

After the show Dad shepherded us around the corner to the Hotel Piccadilly as he played air trombone and whistled "76 Trombones." The Piccadilly, where the Marriott Marquis Hotel now stands, had once been one of the most fashionable hotels in the Theater District, but by the early-'60s it had fallen out of favor and taken on a sad and slightly seedy mien. Beneath the lobby's coffered ceiling and ornate chandeliers, the brocaded sofas and armchairs were faded and the oriental rugs were fraying. Even the potted palms looked tired.

But Dad didn't bring us to the Piccadilly to admire the decor. We were there to dine at the Scandia Restaurant, billed as "New York's smorgasbord delight." Never had an advertising slogan been truer, at least in this boy's eyes. A long buffet table in the middle of the room was arrayed with platters of roast beef, smoked salmon, sturgeon, and other delicacies, punctuated by a murmuring fountain in the center. A ceramic Viking ship stocked with chilled shrimp stood at one end of the table, while lobsters dangled from a pyramid-like display, as if they were growing on a tree, at the other.

As I prepared to launch my initial assault Dad tugged on my shirtsleeve and whispered a familiar refrain in my ear: "Don't be a *fresser!*" Undeterred, I made a beeline for the buffet as if I were a contestant on the TV game show *Supermarket Sweep* and had only five minutes to race around the store and fill my shopping cart. After my fourth or fifth sortie, Dad had seen enough. He snagged me by the ear lobe and indecorously escorted me out of the restaurant. On the drive home I experienced none of the Merritt's magic. I slept all the way, no doubt dreaming of shrimp boats and lobster trees.

Fiddler on the Roof, with Herschel Barnardi playing the role of the pious milkman Tevye, was another family favorite. Driving home after that show, Dad, Richard, and I sang the songs one after the other – "Sunrise, Sunset," "Tradition," "Anatevka." The next morning Dad waltzed into the kitchen as Mom was preparing breakfast and began singing: *If I were a rich man .... Yubby dibby dibby dibby dibby dibby dibby dum,* as he did a Tevya-like dance, twisting his hands in the air and pirouetting. Richard and I laughed and clapped, but when he tried to get Mom to join him on the dance floor, she just smiled and shook her head. I wonder if that song had a special resonance for him because he *had* been a rich man once – but that was a long time ago.

The show that made the deepest impression on me had no words at all. It was a performance by the French mime Marcel Marceau. From the moment he shuffled onto the stage in his signature striped sailor shirt and dark vest, white bell-bottom trousers, and floppy top hat crowned with a droopy red flower, I was completely in his thrall. With his exaggerated movements and facial expressions accentuated by white-face, black eyeliner, and bright red lipstick, Marceau conjured entire worlds out of thin air. One moment he was a fearful lion tamer, the next a tremulous tightrope walker or an enchanted birdkeeper. I was so immersed in his imaginary universe that when the house lights came on at intermission it was the theater itself that seemed unreal.

SHOWROOM

One summer day when I was around 13 or 14 Dad brought me to his showroom in the Garment District in New York. I had been looking forward to the trip for weeks, relishing the opportunity to have a serious man-to-man and heart-to-heart on the two-hour train ride to New York. But as soon as we pulled out of Union Station in New Haven he snapped open the *Times* and by the time we hit Bridgeport, a half-hour down the line, he was snoring like a locomotive, leaving me to admire the scenery. He didn't wake up until the train whooshed into the Park Avenue tunnel at East 97th Street, his eyes popping open as if they were wired to an electronic timer.

I always wondered how Dad managed to deal with his long workdays. Now I knew his secret. I suppose I shouldn't have been surprised because I inherited his gift – or curse, depending on how you look at it – of being able to fall asleep virtually anywhere and anytime. I have been known to nod off on trains, planes, buses, and subways, not to mention at movies, concerts, and plays. The more expensive the ticket, it seems, the more likely I am to succumb to sleep.

The train rolled to a halt at Grand Central with a gentle thud. After a momentary pause, the doors flew open and the battalion of briefcase-armed men, along with a few women, surged out. Dad grabbed my hand as we joined the stampede down the dimly lit platform. As we emerged into the cavernous maw of the Main Concourse, I was momentarily blinded by the shafts of light streaming down from the arched windows in the vaulted ceiling. Random snippets of conversations bounced off the marble walls, piercing the din.

Dad tightened his grip as we wove through the crush of commuters scurrying in all directions and made our way to the Times Square shuttle. We came to ground at Seventh Avenue and 40th Street amid a cacophony of blaring horns, squealing brakes, and barking street vendors and walked south toward the Garment District.

Everything about New York was bigger, faster, louder, messier. Brown-skinned men rolled racks of plastic-covered garments and carts with long rolls of fabric through the streets, singing and cursing as they dodged cars and pedestrians. Tall, angular women in high heels teetered down the sidewalk, alongside harried-looking men in rumpled suits. The frenzy of activity was both exhilarating and frightening, so different from the sedate suburban world I was accustomed to.

Dad was different, too. He nimbly navigated the crowded sidewalks, walking with a confidence and purpose I had rarely seen before. Rather than shrinking from the tumult around him, he seemed to grow bigger and more self-assured. At home my mother ruled with unchallenged supremacy, but here in New York, outside my mother's force field, Dad was in command. This was his domain, and he clearly relished it. It was almost as if he were liberated by all the energy around him.

We entered a hulking skyscraper clad in green brick and pinkish marble on Broadway between 39th and 38th Street and rode the elevator to the 18th floor. I followed Dad down a long corridor to a door with "Crown Shirts Inc." imprinted in small black letters on the frosted glass panel. He gave his bowtie a quick twist and walked in without knocking.

A Black woman with big hair and magenta lipstick was sitting behind a narrow desk. A beige touch-tone phone with several rows of buttons and a circular Rolodex sat on the desk in front of her. She had smooth, caramel-colored skin and large brown eyes, accentuated by long eyelashes and thick eyeliner. She was looking at a magazine and filing her fingernails, which matched the color of her lips. They were the longest nails I had ever seen.

"Good morning, Mr. Cooper," she sang out in a lilting West Indian accent. There was a familiarity in her voice that I found both intriguing and a little disconcerting.

"Good morning, Jacqueline."

"I see you brought an assistant with you this morning," she said, with a smile that revealed a set of dazzling white teeth.

"This is son No. 2. Peter."

"Nice to meet you, Peter," she said, extending a long, slender arm festooned with a clutch of clinking bracelets.

I was more than a little amazed that my father had such a glamorous secretary. Jacqueline looked like she had just stepped out of the pages of *Vogue*. My father, I was beginning to realize, had a life – a big, interesting life – outside our sleepy suburban world.

Jacqueline handed Dad a stack of letters and reminded him that he had an appointment with a buyer in the afternoon. He spent the rest of the morning going through his mail and making phone calls while I occupied myself reading magazines, writing letters on the office stationery, and examining the blouse samples arranged on a round, Formica-topped table in the center of the room. Every so often I would steal a glance at the exotic creature at the front desk as she fielded phone calls and filed those wondrously long nails.

Around 12:30 Dad announced it was time for lunch. We rode the elevator to the ground floor and went into the coffee shop off the lobby, which was packed with businessmen and secretaries jockeying for seats.

"We got no tables," said a bald, burly man behind the cash register, pointing to a pair of stools at the far end of the counter. We squeezed into our seats and looked over a long laminated menu offering a dizzying assortment of sandwiches, platters, side dishes, and beverages. After a few minutes a big-breasted waitress wearing a pair of tear-shaped rhinestone-studded glasses appeared in front of us.

"What'll it be, sweetheart?" she said, clicking her gum and looking at Dad as if he were an old chum from high school. I was struck by the intimacy of her greeting. Did she actually know my father, I wondered, or did she greet all her male customers that way?

"What's good today?" Dad replied in an equally casual tone that did nothing to solve the riddle.

"What do you feel like, hon? Saul made a nice meatloaf this morning." She waited a beat as Dad continued perusing the menu. "You can't go wrong with the chicken salad," she tried again, as she looked around impatiently.

"Give me the corned beef on rye with a cup of coffee."

"Good choice," she said, unconvincingly, as she jotted the order down. "You want potato salad or slaw with that?" He went with the potato salad.

"And what about you, young man?" she continued, looking down at me as if I were a mildly interesting science project. Overwhelmed by all the choices, I opted for my old standby: egg salad on white with lettuce, tomato, and onion, and a chocolate egg cream.

When we returned to the showroom after lunch a man with a big, bushy mustache was sitting at a desk in the back talking on the phone in a clipped Long Island accent. He glanced up at Dad and waved. *OK, OK. Right, right, right. So I got you down for 25 blue, 25 pink, and 25 mixed. What else? OK. Right, right, right. You got it.*

The man went on like that for several minutes, jotting down orders with a pencil on a small notepad, before slamming down the phone and muttering something under his breath. He stood up, revealing a tall, lanky frame clad in a slightly-too-large suit. His longish brown hair was slicked back, accentuating his receding hairline and prominent hooked nose.

"Mr. Cooper," he said with an exaggerated bow. "And who have we here?" he added, looking down at me with a toothy smile.

"This is son number two," Dad repeated. "Pete, this is our top salesman, Herb Cohen."

"Your top salesman who just wrote up 200 dozen pieces for

Caldor's," Herb proclaimed, as he patted me on the head like I was a pet poodle.

It was hard not to notice how different these two men were. Dad was dressed in a drab olive-colored suit with narrow lapels, a pale yellow button-down shirt, and a bowtie. Herb, on the other hand, was wearing a loud plaid suit with mile-wide lapels, a bright pink shirt, and a red tie that fluttered like the jib of a sailboat. Dad's low, soft growl was almost inaudible, while Herb's high-pitched, nasally voice bounced off the walls. The only thing the two men seemed to have in common was they were both Jews who worked in the *schmatta* trade.

On the train home, as Dad puffed on a Montecristo in the smoking car and flipped though the *Post*, I reflected on the day's events. My father, I discovered, was having a secret love affair – with New York City. In big, blustery Manhattan he was not the meek, acquiescent man I knew at home. He was the boss, decisive and purposeful, the master of his own fate. I liked my old Dad well enough, but I liked this new one even better.

DRUGS, DEADHEADS, AND DIVINE LIGHT

It's hard to imagine two people more different than my father and brother. Dad was a quiet traditionalist who played by the rules and didn't like to draw attention to himself. His elder son, in contrast, was an irreverent free spirit who enjoyed flouting convention. As one of his childhood friends once told me, "Richard lived on the edge before any of us even knew what that meant."

My brother's rebellious nature was apparent from an early age. In junior high he spent nearly as much time in the assistant principal's office, where he was regularly dispatched for misconduct, as he did in class. His decorum didn't improve in high school, where he made a habit of skipping class to smoke smoke pot with his friends in the woods behind the football field. After getting his driver's license he wasted little time collecting a spate of speeding tickets while inflicting an assortment of dings, scrapes, and more serious insults on Mom's Impala.

Desperate for a course correction, my parents pulled Richard out of Hamden High and send him to Williston Academy, a prep school in the Berkshires. But rather than rein him in, Williston's starchy culture only seemed to fuel his mutinous spirit. He let his thick black hair grow into a gnarly nest and spent his free time holed up in his room smoking weed and teaching himself to play the guitar.

After (somehow) graduating from Williston, he enrolled in Lafayette College, Uncle Mac's alma mater. By then the '60s counterculture was in full flower and Richard eagerly embraced many of its customs. He wore his hair in a ponytail, dressed in frayed bellbottoms and ratty T-shirts, and began experimenting with LSD, mescaline, and other hallucinogenics. He spent endless hours listening to the Grateful Dead and, like other Deadheads, thought nothing of hitchhiking hundreds of miles to catch one of their shows.

One night, around 2 a.m., my parents got a call from Richard. He was in a phonebooth somewhere in New Jersey, but he didn't know exactly where he was or how he had gotten there because he was tripping on LSD. Dad managed to coax enough clues out of his muddled musings to enable the State Police to track him down. I didn't find out about the unfolding drama until my parents woke me up in the middle of the night to tell me they were driving to Jersey to pick him up at the police station.

During another trip gone bad, my mother got a call from a neighbor reporting that she had spotted Richard hitchhiking on Whitney Avenue, a few blocks from our house. Something didn't seem right, she said. My mother raced down the hill to find her elder son in a catatonic state, a blank expression on his face and his thumb frozen in the air. He was taken by ambulance to Yale-New Haven Hospital, where he was committed to the psychiatric unit for several weeks of observation and treatment. The doctors prescribed a medication called tryptophan, which left him in a perpetual state of drowsiness. The treatment inspired him to compose a ditty he called "The Tryptophan Shuffle," which he played zestfully on his guitar to the amusement of the other patients and their visitors.

It was around this time that Richard got involved with Divine Light Mission, a religious group led by a pudgy 13-year-old Indian boy who dubbed himself Guru Maharaj Ji. At first my parents didn't take his involvement with the group very seriously, but as he spent more and more time attending DLM programs, their concern grew. At Richard's invitation, I reluctantly attended one of these events, which was held in a field in rural Connecticut. As the round-faced swami sat on a plush chair on a makeshift stage, hundreds of his devotees sat cross-legged on the ground, blissfully beaming up at him. Speaking in a soft singsong inflected with an occasional high-pitched squeal, the guru rambled on, and on, about inner peace, love, and light. Each banal parable and vapid truism was greeted with ripples of delighted laughter by his rapt audience.

I was mystified that a smart guy like Richard could be taken in by what I viewed as, at best, pseudo spirituality and, at worst, a colossal scam, but when I expressed my skepticism after the program his mood darkened and he quickly cut off the conversation. It was a pattern I saw repeated often over the years: Whenever my parents or I challenged him about the guru or his beliefs, he would shut down and retreat to some inner sanctum where he couldn't be reached.

After graduating from Lafayette, Richard moved into a DLM ashram in a rambling old house on Whitney Avenue in New Haven, not far from where we grew up on Willow Street. Like other *premies*, as the Guru's devotees were called, he worked at odd jobs, painting houses and building cabinets, and turned over all his earnings to the group.

Dad rarely spoke about Richard's association with the DLM, but one can imagine the dismay he must have felt. After narrowly escaping an antisemitic butcher who murdered his father and millions of other Jews, he witnessed his first-born son, bar mitzvahed a few years earlier, disavow his Jewish faith and embrace an obscure Indian mystic barely old enough to drive.[1]

GAY BOY

One weekend afternoon when I was about 15 or 16 Dad took me to a movie at the Lincoln Theatre, a fusty art house near the Yale campus. I don't recall the name of the movie or even what it was about, but one moment jumped out at me – a brief, shadowy scene showing two men kissing. I tried not to react, but my palms turned clammy as my fingernails dug into the frayed velvet armrests.

"Animals," Dad muttered under his breath as we were leaving the theater. I wasn't sure if he was referring to the movie in general or to the gay kiss, but the remark sent a cold slick of sweat down my spine. I took it as confirmation of my worst fears: that my father was repulsed by homosexuality and, therefore, would be repulsed by his own son.

I'm not sure when I first became aware of my attraction to other boys. When I was about seven or eight a friend and I got caught by his mother playing doctor in our underwear in the basement of their house. She immediately marched me home and ratted me out to my mother, who banished me to my room for the rest of the afternoon. Mom never mentioned the incident again, but she didn't have to. I felt as if I had committed some terrible sin, though I wasn't sure exactly what it was. I was never allowed to play at that friend's house again. Come to think of it, I was never invited back.

There were other signs that might have given my parents pause. When I was six or seven, I slipped into their bedroom, donned my mother's pearl necklace, rhinestone earrings, and high heels and teetered into the living room, arms akimbo, to show off my new ensemble. Dad looked up from his newspaper and erupted in a guttural laugh, but Mom wasn't so amused.

"*Vey iz mir!*" she wailed.[1] "Take that off this minute, Peter! And don't you dare go into Mommy's things again!"

Another clue about my sexual orientation might have been my penchant for singing and dancing around the house to the soundtracks of Broadway musicals. *South Pacific*, *Oliver!* and *Fiddler on the Roof* were three of my favorites, but the show that gave me the biggest kick was *West Side Story*. I got goosebumps listening to Bernstein's big, lyrical score and those tough-talking, finger-snapping Jets and Sharks only added to the allure. I played the album over and over again on our RCA portable record player as I twirled around the den belting out "Maria," "Tonight," and – most problematic, perhaps, from my parents' perspective – "I Feel Pretty." At first they found my performances amusing, but after a while the album mysteriously disappeared.

And then there was my infatuation with Judy Garland. From the moment I first saw *The Wizard of Oz*, I couldn't get enough of her or her music – a not uncommon phenomenon among gay men.[2] What must my parents (and the neighbors) have thought of my penchant for sitting on the curb in front of our house warbling "Somewhere Over the Rainbow" off key and *ad nauseum*.

In junior high I took to sneaking into my parents' bathroom before school to experiment with my mother's cosmetics. I dabbed my cheeks with rouge and rubbed coverup on my lips. I thought my makeover was quite subtle and sophisticated, but one morning as I sat down to breakfast Dad turned to me and squinted.

"What's that on your face?" he asked.

My rouged cheeks no doubt turned several shades redder. "Nothing," I mumbled as I lowered my face to my plate and shoveled in a forkful of eggs. After scarfing down the rest of my breakfast I raced into the bathroom and scrubbed my face until it burned.

I dreaded going to gym. Just the thought of undressing in front of the other boys made my stomach flutter with anxiety. I was deeply ashamed of my skeletal body, but even more distressing, I was terrified of getting a hard-on. To avoid that possibility, I usually tried to sneak out of the locker room without taking a shower, but the gym teacher, Mr. D'Angelo, a Charles Atlas lookalike with bulging muscles and a granite chin, got wise to me. "Where do you think you're going, bar mitzvah boy?" he would call out in his booming voice, prompting snickers from the other boys.

My parents never discussed the birds and the bees with me. About the closest they came to addressing the subject was when they presented me with a copy of *Everything You Always Wanted to Know About Sex* *But Were Afraid to Ask*[3] for Hanukkah one year. The bright yellow paperback appeared sometime in the middle of the eight-day holiday, after the real presents in the first few nights but before the Hershey bars, oranges, and dreidels that typically came toward the end.

Of course I immediately looked up the chapter on homosexuality, which only served to confuse me even more. The author, Dr. David Reuben, explained that sex between men primarily occurred in public bathrooms and involved "no feeling, no sentiment, no nothing." He described a typical encounter this way: "A homosexual walks into the men's washroom and spots another homosexual. One drops to his knees, the other unzips his pants, and a few moments later it's over. No names, no faces, no emotions." Given the impersonal nature of these trysts, the good doctor opined, homosexuals might do better having sex with "a masturbation machine." Not exactly a ringing endorsement.

Homosexuality was a taboo subject in our house, and when it did come up it was usually out of earshot of the *kinda*. One afternoon I overheard Mom and Aunt Nan talking about the husband of a prominent local politician who had been arrested at a roadside rest stop for soliciting sex with other men.

"What a *shonda*," Mom hissed, employing the Yiddish term for shame. "It's a sickness."

"That poor woman," Nan added, shaking her head. "What she must be going through. And he always seemed like such a *mensch*."

PART III

LOST PORTRAITS

Several weeks after returning from my first visit to Weiden in 1979, I received a letter from Inge with some "wonderful news." She had been contacted by an elderly woman named Emma Fischer who had been a housekeeper in my grandfather's house for many years. Frau Fischer told her that when the Nazis forced Otto and Mina to sell the villa in 1939, they asked her to safeguard a pair of oil paintings of their parents, Eduard and Franziska, until they could come back to reclaim them.

Frau Fischer had kept the portraits ever since, carefully packed in layers of cotton wool and cloth, hoping to return them one day to a member of Dad's family. Unfortunately, being 90 years old and nearly blind, she didn't learn about my visit to Weiden until after I had left. Now, she told Inge, she would like nothing more than to return the paintings to their rightful owner.

Inge's letter included a copy of a nearly full-page article she had written in *Der Neue Tag* about Fischer and the paintings. Under the headline "Zwei Wertvolle Gemälde für Peter Cooper" [Two Valuable Paintings for Peter Cooper], the story described how she has been "guarding" the portraits of Eduard and Fanni for more than 40 years and looked forward to presenting them as "a gift for their great-grandchildren." The article was accompanied by a photograph of a handsome old woman with neatly coiffed gray hair sitting on a couch holding up the portraits, one in each hand, as she gazes at the camera with a sad smile and sunken eyes.

I immediately wrote to Frau Fischer, thanking her for taking care of the paintings all these years and expressing my desire to meet her and reclaim them for my family. A few weeks later I received her response: "It would be a pleasure to give you these pictures in person. I would like to speak to you personally because I have so much to say to you." Had she known that I had been in town and was staying at the youth hostel, she added, "I would have offered you my apartment and it will always be open to you."

Unfortunately, I wasn't able to return to Weiden for nearly four years. By then Frau Fischer had died and the portraits had been inherited by her niece, a woman I'll call Frau S.

Inge met me at the train station on a balmy late August afternoon, greeting me like a long-lost friend. "Hallo Peter!" she said, smiling warmly as she gave me a firm handshake (a hug, were she inclined to give me one, would have been awkward because I was wearing a backpack). "Welcome back to Weiden!"

As we drove to her house for dinner, Inge filled me in on the latest developments in the saga of Eduard and Fanni. After Frau Fischer died, Inge had contacted her niece, whom she described as "one of the poorest people in town." At first Frau S. refused to give up the paintings, but she changed her mind after the head of the Catholic diocese, at Inge's behest, made a personal appeal.

Inge lived in a modest house in a quiet neighborhood on the outskirts of town. She introduced me to her daughter, Doris, who, like her mother, was tall and attractive, but unlike Inge, was painfully shy. We were joined for dinner by Inge's boyfriend, an English engineer, also named Peter, who was working on a project to build a pump station on the Czech border for a Soviet gas pipeline. He was short and stocky with a sharply receding hairline, not the type of guy

I imagined Inge would be with, but he was a friendly bloke with a ribald sense of humor.

After dinner we were joined by a friend of Inge's named Dieter, the manager of a local hotel, and his cocker spaniel Casimar. Dieter was an exuberant raconteur who entertained us with stories about his guests, many of whom were Americans associated with a US military base in the adjoining town of Grafenwöhr. Around 11 p.m., after consuming numerous glasses of Campari, Riesling, and Hefeweizen, it was decided that we would reconvene at Dieter's hotel for a nightcap. I was exhausted after a long day of travel, but I didn't want to be a party pooper. Besides, Dieter – at Inge's suggestion – had invited me to be his guest at the hotel, so there was no easy way out.

The bar at the Hotel Stadtkrug was swarming with Americans, both military and civilian, and it seemed as if every one of them wanted to buy me a drink. It was well past midnight by the time Peter drove Inge and Doris home, leaving me in the hands of Dieter and his attentive staff. When Peter returned he insisted on pouring me a glass of whiskey from a "special bottle" he had brought from Scotland. After a couple of shots I excused myself and stumbled into the bathroom. The next thing I knew Dieter and Peter were carrying me up the stairs to my room. Apparently I had passed out on the toilet. Left to my own devices, I promptly was sick, took a cold shower, and collapsed into bed.

I woke up the next morning with a throbbing headache and a queasy stomach and staggered downstairs for breakfast. Inge came by to collect me for our appointment with Frau S. Judging from the concerned expression on her face, she had already been informed about the indecorous denouement of my evening. "Peter, are you OK?" she asked as she peered into my bloodshot eyes. "You look a little tired."

After assuring her I was fine, we walked a few blocks to Frau S.'s apartment, which was located on the second floor of a run-down brick building in a slightly seedy part of town. We were greeted by an unsmiling middle-aged woman with lank grayish-blonde hair. Frau S. led us into a dusty room crowded with heavy pieces of furniture. Two long sofas faced each other across a low coffee table cluttered with old newspapers, magazines, and dirty dishes. She gestured for us to sit on one couch while she perched on the arm of the other.

The two women began talking in rapid-fire German. I couldn't understand exactly what they were saying but I could tell from the increasingly strident tone that things were not going according to plan. Apparently S. had had a change of heart. Yes, she would turn over the paintings, but only for a price – 30,000 DM (deutschmarks), which was equivalent to about $12,000 – a sum she claimed was based on an appraisal by a Munich art dealer.

Inge tried to reason with her, pointing out that my grandfather had entrusted the portraits to her aunt with the understanding that she would return them after the war. Moreover, Frau Fischer had clearly stated in her letter to me that she intended to give me the paintings. Besides, Inge pointed out, who would willingly give away portraits of their own parents?

After failing to gain traction with any of these arguments and barely able to contain her exasperation, Inge warned: "If you keep these paintings, they will bring bad karma on you and your family!"

But S. was unmoved. She insisted the paintings belonged to her and that she desperately needed the money. Her husband suffered from schizophrenia and alcoholism and could not hold a job, and she was obliged to support him as well as their grown son, who was also unemployed.

"I haven't had a vacation in years," she said plaintively, "and I plan to use the money to take one." Besides, she added, casting a sharp glance in my direction, I came from a wealthy family and could well afford it.

Even if the latter were true, which it wasn't, there was no way I was going to pay her even a pfennig. The paintings belonged to my family, after all, and had ended up in her hands only because of Nazi persecution. As far as I was concerned, she was nothing more than a common thief. Moreover, according to an appraiser Inge had consulted, the portraits were worth only a fraction of what S. claimed. They were unremarkable, unsigned examples of the Viennese school of painting with a market value of no more than 10,000 DM, or about $2,000 each.

On the way to S.'s apartment, Inge and I had discussed the possibility of offering her a modest sum, perhaps few thousand marks, as a token of appreciation for surrendering the paintings, but she was demanding 10 times that amount.

While the two women were talking a gaunt, disheveled man wandered into the room. S. introduced him as her husband. Herr S. offered us a damp hand to shake but didn't say a word. It was clear he wasn't well. He padded nervously back and forth across the living room, shaking his head and gulping for air. Then a slovenly-looking young man came in and silently went into the kitchen. I assumed this was S.'s son, but Inge told me later it was a boarder she had taken in to help pay the bills.

Not only did S. refuse to give up the paintings, but she wouldn't even allow me to see them, claiming they were being kept in a "secret" location outside of Weiden.

When it became clear that she wasn't going to change her mind, Inge signaled me that it was time to go. We got up and left without shaking hands or even saying goodbye.

"A terrible person," Inge said, nearly in tears, as we walked back to her car.

We drove to the mayor's office, which was now located in a modern new office building around the corner from *Der Neue Tag*. I received a much warmer reception this time than I had during my first visit to Weiden. Clearly, being accompanied by a prominent local journalist has its advantages. We were promptly ushered into the office of the *Oberbürgermeister,* Hans Schröpf, a well-fed middle-aged man with a round face and dark hair streaked with gray.

After Inge explained the situation, the mayor promised to talk to S. himself. He also said the city might be willing to provide some funds – perhaps 2,000 or 3,000 DM – to persuade her to surrender the paintings.

Later that afternoon my old friend Eduard Wittmann came by Inge's house to see me. He had sprouted a few more white hairs since I last saw him, but other than that he was the same gregarious, good-humored man I remembered. Eddie said that he, too, had spoken to S. and had offered her several thousand marks to give up the paintings. He had also discussed the situation with the local chapter of the Lions Club, of which he was a member, and the club was prepared to offer S. a monthly pension in addition to a lump sum payment if she agreed to hand over the paintings.

Further appeals were made by local religious leaders as well as by an official with the trade union representing local glass workers. But Frau S., apparently still convinced that I was the American scion of a wealthy German industrialist who could well afford to pay the price she demanded, rebuffed them all.

The next night I had dinner with Eddie at the Stadtkrug. As usual he ordered nothing but the best, and plenty of it, including a good bottle of Riesling. He presented me with a porcelain ash tray made by his company commemorating 300 years of German-American friendship. I was touched by his thoughtfulness and grateful to have a friend like him in Dad's hometown. It almost felt like he had become a surrogate father, a feeling that was reinforced by something he shared at dinner. He told me that he and wife had no children because she was incapable of giving birth. The uncharacteristic grimace on his normally smiling face made it clear that this was still a painful subject.

After dinner we took a stroll through Marktplatz, past the colorful, centuries-old gabled houses lining the square, as Eddie held forth on the history of the city. It crossed my mind that Dad had no doubt walked the same cobbled plaza many times as a young man. We stopped at a restaurant near the Altes Rathaus for dessert. As we were leaving Eddie stopped to chat with an elderly couple he knew. When he introduced me, the man gave me a quizzical look. "Kupfer?" he said. "Yes, yes, I remember your family." He was about to say something else, but after glancing at his wife he abruptly fell silent. I was eager to know how he knew Dad's family, but I got the impression he didn't want to say anything more, so I didn't ask.

The next morning I called the US Consulate in Munich to ask if they could help me get the paintings back. The woman I spoke to was sympathetic but said there wasn't much they could do unless I had proof that the paintings had belonged to my family and had been given to Frau Fischer temporarily for safekeeping. And even then, she noted, it would most likely involve a long and costly legal process.

That afternoon I had lunch with Hardy and Gabi, the young couple I had met during my first visit to Weiden, who were now married. Their wedding had been a major event for the Jewish community in the area because it was the first one held at the old synagogue in Floss since it was painstakingly reconstructed after nearly being destroyed on Kristallnacht.

Floss had been a center of Jewish life for centuries, but not a single Jew lived there any longer. Hardy and Gabi were afraid the Jewish community in Weiden would suffer the same fate. There were only about 30 or 35 Jews left in the city, they explained, compared with more than 170 before the war. The synagogue did not have enough members to support a full-time rabbi, so a visiting rabbi was brought in for holidays and special occasions. Hardy's younger brother, Michael, had been the only Jewish pupil in his public school and last student to get Jewish religion lessons there.[1]

Gabi told me that when she was in school, in the early-1970s, little attention was paid to the Nazi era and the Holocaust. "It was taught like any other subject, as if it were ancient history," she recalled. That echoed something Inge had told me earlier. When she was a girl, in the years immediately after the war, the Holocaust wasn't even mentioned in school. She suspected one reason was that many of the teachers and school administrators had been Nazis themselves. It was only much later that Germany began to come to terms with its Nazi past and children were taught the terrible truth about what happened. Today, teaching about the Holocaust and the Nazi regime is mandatory in German schools, and most students are required to visit a concentration camp or a Holocaust memorial, though some educators believe more should be done to inform young Germans about that monstrous chapter in their nation's history.

After lunch we visited Hardy's father, Hermann Brenner, the president of the synagogue, at his fabric shop on Marktplatz. A soft-spoken man neatly dressed in a suit and tie, I felt an immediate affinity with him because he reminded me of my father in both his appearance and manner. Although he didn't speak much English, his words radiated a calm I found familiar and reassuring.

The next day, my last in Weiden, I met Hardy's brother Michael, who had recently published a book about Jewish life in Weiden under the Nazis.[2] The book had grown out of a national writing competition on German history he had won while he was in high school. Much of the material was based on the recollections of former Jewish residents Michael had tracked down in Israel, the US, and other countries.

Shortly before Frau Fischer died, Inge had arranged for a professional photographer to make reproductions of Eduard and Fanni's portraits. She was concerned that something might happen to the old woman, or to the paintings themselves, and she wanted me to at least have copies. She sent me a pair of 5x7 color reproductions, which I framed and set on a shelf in my living room, next to a picture of Dad. Typical of Inge, she paid for everything and refused to take a dime from me. he visited my mother and me in Connecticut several years later when he was working on his Ph.D. at Columbia University

Now that it appeared the portraits of Eduard and Fanni would not be reunited with their family after all, I was even more grateful for Inge's foresight and thoughtfulness. The reproductions, it seemed, were all I would have to remember my great grandparents.

Emma Fischer holding Portraits of Fanni and Eduard

THE QUEST

The discovery of Eduard and Fanni's portraits rekindled my curiosity about my father and his family, a quest that has now spanned more than four decades and several continents. In an effort to piece together their story, I have traveled to his hometown in Bavaria five times; visited or viewed files from Holocaust centers in Washington, Berlin, Paris, London, and Jerusalem and German government archives in Munich and Wiesbaden; and corresponded with numerous government agencies, nonprofit organizations, and private individuals in the US and Germany.

My research has been hampered by the fact that I don't speak German, so I've had to rely on the kindness of friends, relatives, and strangers to translate and explain a lot of the material. Foremost among these is my cousin Paul in England,[1] a retired lawyer who is fluent in German and was a volunteer at the Weiner Library for the Study of the Holocaust and Genocide in London; Dr. Sebastian Schott, director of the Weiden Office of Culture, Urban History, and Tourism, who wrote a dissertation about the Jewish community of Weiden;[2] and my German-American friend Franziska Marks.

Robert Charles Kupfer was born in Weiden on December 8, 1906. He and his older brother Ernst lived with their parents in a series of apartments near their grandparents' house, the stone manor across from the railroad station known in town as the Kupfer villa. The extended Kupfer clan, which was scattered across Bavaria and Bohemia between Frankfurt and Vienna, often gathered at the villa for holidays and other occasions. Dad's album contains several photographs of family members posing outside the house, the men nattily dressed in suits and ties, the women in simple dresses or skirts and sweaters, the children in lederhosen or sailor outfits.

My father never got to know his grandfather Eduard, the patriarch of the family, who died in February 1907, two months after Dad was born. After his death, Fanni continued living in the villa along with two of her adult daughters, Hermine Klein and Johanna Rosenwald. Mina and her son Paul had moved in with her mother after getting divorced – a rare, possibly scandalous, event in those days – and Johanna, or Hani, joined them after her husband died.

The Holocaust was, of course, the great trauma of my father's early life, but he lived through another momentous event that surely had a big impact on him and his family: World War I. He was seven years old when Germany entered the war in August 1914. By the time the fighting ended four years later, more than 2 million Germans had been killed and 4.1 million wounded, out of a total population of 65 million. One of the casualties was Dad's cousin Paul Klein, who was a 21-year-old soldier in the Bavarian Army when he was killed in 1915 – the lone Jewish war victim from Weiden.[3]

My grandfather Otto also served in the Bavarian Army during the war. Typical of Dad, he never mentioned his father's military service to me.[4] Given Otto's age – he was 41 when the conflict began – and his occupation as a factory director, he probably served in an administrative capacity rather than a combat role. Even so, it's likely he was away from home a good deal, leaving his wife Berta, 10 years his junior, in charge of running the household.

In the fall of 1916, at age nine, Dad entered the Weiden *Realschule*, which prepared students for a commercial occupation.⁵ He was one of only three Jewish students in a class of 48, most of whom were Catholic.⁶

It was a difficult time for Germany. An Allied blockade had cut off imports of food, resulting in widespread malnutrition and starvation. The winter of 1916-1917 was called "turnip winter" because a poor potato harvest had forced many Germans to eat turnips and other crops typically reserved for farm animals. Frequent strikes by workers seeking better pay and working conditions only added to the economic pain.

To what extent my father and his family struggled during the war is hard to say. Given that they were relatively affluent, it would be safe to assume they suffered less than the average German family. Still, shortages of food and other supplies and restrictions on travel and other activities, not to mention a general state of anxiety weighing on any nation at war, must have taken a toll.

Dad graduated from the *Realschule* in 1922, when he was 15, and moved to Düsseldorf to work as an apprentice at a metal wholesaler owned by an in-law of his mother's named Eugen Wetzler. Among Dad's papers is a letter from Wetzler lauding his performance in a series of jobs in the shipping, accounting, and warehousing departments. "Through his tireless diligence, his great punctuality, his clean, precise handwriting, and his zeal in the exercise of our business interests, Robert Kupfer gained our great satisfaction, which we expressed by repeatedly increasing his responsibilities and his corresponding salary after the first few months of employment," Wetzler wrote. "He has always carried out the bookkeeping tasks assigned to him particularly accurately and reliably, has shorthand and is an advanced typist."

A year later, in November 1923, Dad abruptly resigned his position and moved back to Weiden. His mother had died of cancer. She was only 40; he was 16. Six months later the family suffered another blow when Fanni, the strong-willed matriarch of the Kupfer clan, died at 77. My father never talked about his mother or grandmother or the impact they had on him, but losing two major figures in his life in quick succession, especially at such a young age, must have left lasting scars.

Dad spent the next three years working with his father at the Weiden *Glasfabrik*. As was the case during his apprenticeship in Düsseldorf, he worked in several different departments, including payroll, accounting, and shipping. According to a reference letter written by Dr. Otto Seeling, director of Tafel, Salin und Spiegelglas Fabriken AG [Sheet, Salt and Mirror Glass Factories Ltd.] in Fürth, the company that succeeded the family glass business after it went public, Dad performed admirably. "Mr. Kupfer carried out the work assigned to him with diligence and zeal and to our fullest satisfaction," he wrote. "He proved a good business talent and a quick learner. These abilities, combined with a great deal of character and good manners, make us hope for the best in his commercial development." In a separate letter, Dr. Seeling directed the payroll department to give Dad "a farewell bonus" of 50 reichsmarks.

In September 1926, when he was 19, Dad moved to Mannheim, in southwest Germany, to continue his business studies. Two years later he relocated again, this time to Cham, a medieval market town 50 miles southeast of Weiden. I found no records of what he did there, but it's likely he was employed at Teller & Klein, a wholesaler of agricultural products co-owned by his mother's father, Ignaz Klein.

Ernst and Dad, circa 1911

Family portrait (Dad on right with dog), circa 1912

Dad with this dog Peter, circa 1914

Kupfer Villa Weiden, circa 1925

GLASS DYNASTY

I knew Dad's family had been in the glass business and had owned a factory in Weiden, but it wasn't until I visited his hometown and began doing research for this book that I came to appreciate the scope of the business and its importance in the region. Much of what I learned is based on the work of Dr. Michael Müller, a retired German economist who has written extensively about the history of the Bavarian glass industry and the role the Kupfers played in it. One article in particular, about an old foundry near the Czech border, provided a wealth of information about the family business.[1]

Jews have been making glass for thousands of years. Indeed, in ancient times glassmaking was considered a Jewish trade because it was believed that only Jews were privy to the secret art of transforming stony silicates into the smooth, transparent material called glass. Through the centuries, as Jews dispersed across the Middle East, North Africa, Asia, and Europe, they brought their knowledge of glassmaking with them. "Wherever the Jews went on their desperate odyssey through the Diaspora, the art of glassmaking went with them," Samuel Kurinsky wrote in his book, *The Glassmakers*.[2]

Among those places were Bavaria and neighboring Bohemia, which has been a center of glassmaking since the Middle Ages. With its dense forests of Scots pine, beech, and spruce veined by rivers and streams, the region was well suited for the task. Trees were an inexpensive source of fuel to fire the foundry furnaces as well as a rich source of potash, a key component of glass. The waterways provided the hydropower to operate the machines used to grind and polish the raw glass.

By the mid-1880s, Bavaria and Bohemia were home to scores of glass foundries and hundreds of finishing works. The superior quality of the glass produced in the region made it popular across Europe and beyond.[3] Many of these businesses were owned by newly emancipated Jews, who saw opportunity in the lucrative and growing industry.[4]

According to Müller, my great-great-grandfather Moses (Moritz) Kupfer, along with his nephew Aloys Kupfer and Hermann Glaser, a relative through marriage, sowed the seeds of a sheet glass dynasty in the early 1800s. Their business activities were concentrated in the Oberpfalz and Bohemia, which was then part of the Austro-Hungarian Empire. They later expanded to other parts of Bavaria as well as to the Salzburg area of Austria and to Galicia, a region straddling the modern-day border between Poland and Ukraine.

At the height of their success, around the turn of the 20th century, the Kupfers and Glasers were one of the largest producers of sheet and mirror glass in the region. Through several partnerships, the family controlled a dozen *Glashütten,* or glass foundries, and 40 to 45 *Schleif und Polierwerken,* or grinding and polishing works.[5] The sprawling enterprise employed nearly 1,000 workers, in addition to dozens of others involved in management and sales.

The Kupfers and Glasers were "among the leading personalities of the industry, respected and accepted far beyond the borders of Bohemia and Bavaria," Müller observed. "For customers and prospective customers, the brand Kupfer & Glaser meant competence and continuity in the sheet and mirror glass business."

To what extent that respect and acceptance extended beyond the sphere of business is hard to say. However, one indication of the family's social stature came near the end of the 19th century when Moritz's son, Eduard, my great-grandfather, was named a

Kommerzienrat, or commercial counselor, an honorary title bestowed by the Bavarian government on businessmen who have made significant contributions to society.

The business was truly a family affair. Foundries and other operations were all managed by family members or close associates. Dozens of Kupfers and Glasers were involved in the business, including four of Eduard's five sons, my grandfather Otto among them, four of Aloys' five sons, and two of Hermann Glaser's five sons.

As was common among Jewish families, personal and professional relationships were often intertwined. In a society where Jews were often excluded, these relationships provided access to financing and, just as important, a means of sharing responsibility and risk within a framework of mutual trust.

At times the intertwining was almost incestuous. There were numerous instances of intermarriage between different branches of the Kupfer and Glaser families. To cite a few examples: my great-grandfather Eduard married Fanni, the daughter of Hermann Glaser. Eduard's first cousin Aloys married two of Eduard's sisters in succession, first Johanna and then, after Johanna died at age 30, Josephine. Hermann Glaser's son Sigmund married Aloys' sister Marie, and another son, Ignaz, married Aloys' daughter Emilie. And so on.

A pivotal event in the family business occurred in 1859 when Moritz and Aloys leased an old foundry in Frankenreuth, a hamlet on the border with Bohemia. Founded in 1487 and reputed to be the oldest *Glashütte* in the Oberpfalz, the Frankenreuth glassworks played a central role in the family's business and personal fortunes over the next 30 years.

In 1864, Aloys moved into Frankenreuth No. 1, the capacious manor house attached to the foundry, where he and his wife raised eight children. The following year Eduard married Fanni in Prague and the newlyweds moved to Frankenreuth, most likely sharing the manor with Aloys and his family.

It must have been a busy household because Eduard and Fanni didn't waste any time making a family of their own. Their first child, Johanna, was born in 1866 – nine months and two weeks after their wedding – and the couple continued to procreate at a rapid clip. Records show Fanni gave birth to a dozen children, two of whom died in infancy.[6] Otto, the couple's fifth child, was born in 1873.

Frankenreuth was, for all intents and purposes, a company town. As was customary with *Glashütten*, the Kupfers provided the workers with free housing. They also made an effort to accommodate the religious needs of the workers, most if not all of whom were Catholic, by restoring the hamlet's diminutive church and installing a large cross inside the foundry.

The relationship between the Christian workers and their Jewish overseers appears to have been amicable and mutually beneficial. The workers were dependent on the glassworks for their economic survival because there were few other jobs in the area, and the Kupfers obviously profited from a stable and satisfied workforce. "The cooperation with the glass workers was clearly characterized by a strict relationship of trust," Müller noted. "They were loyal to the patriarchs, the guarantors of their employment and landlords of their accommodation."

Through the 1880s and 1890s, the family glass business grew rapidly. The general business model was to take over existing foundries and modernize and expand them. By 1897 the firms of Kupfer & Glaser and E. & A. Kupfer (Edward and Aloys) controlled three foundries and 20 grinding and polishing works in Bavaria and nine foundries and 20 to 25 finishing works in Austria-Hungary. Kupfer & Glaser was responsible for sales in Austria-Hungary, while E. & A. Kupfer managed sales in Bavaria, elsewhere in Western Europe, and overseas.

The year 1892 marked another milestone in the family business. E. & A. Kupfer purchased a glass factory in Weiden, a city of about 6,000 people 20 miles west of Frankenreuth, from the brothers Heinrich and Karl Schulz. The deal included a coal-fired smelting plant, two apartment houses, and a sizeable amount of land. The Schulzes had built the foundry only the year before to take advantage of a new railroad line running through Weiden, but they apparently ran into financial problems. A few years later, in 1900, Eduard and his family moved to Weiden, occupying a large house befitting a prosperous industrialist down the street from the factory.

The Kupfers immediately set about making improvements to the Weiden *Glasfabrik*, installing a new furnace and power plant and building a spur linking the factory to the nearby rail line. Electric power was installed in 1897. Additional housing was built for the workers and other amenities were provided, including a butcher, a canteen, and a bakery. By the onset of World War I, in 1914, the factory was one of the largest industries in Weiden, employing some 260 workers.

"Without a doubt the members of the Kupfer family were among the most outstanding business people of the Jewish citizens of Weiden," Dr. Schott wrote in his thesis on the city's Jewish community. "They made a contribution to the safeguarding and development of the glass industry that can scarcely be underestimated."

The year 1899 was another watershed for the Kupfer-Glaser glass empire, according to Müller. The firm of E. & A. Kupfer was disbanded and Eduard and Aloys Kupfer and Sigmund Glaser divided the company's assets. The breakup came "as a result of an amicable agreement," according to an official announcement, but there is evidence to suggest that the parting was not all sweetness and light.

Over the preceding half century, the Kupfers and Glasers had built a business enterprise that was "remarkable for its time," Müller observed, but by 1899 the company was under financial duress and seriously undercapitalized. Sigmund's brother Ignaz Glaser summed up the situation this way: "They had run a substantial business for 25 years without ever accounting between themselves. They imagined they had millions and yet were unable to pay the most pressing debts."[7]

A balance sheet for August 1, 1898 showed the company had capital roughly equivalent to $3 million in today's dollars, which was considered far too small for a business its size. A reasonable value, according to Müller, would have been six times that amount. "The trust which had kept the three partners together for decades was now quickly lost," he noted. "The end of their collaboration and a division of the assets of the business had become inevitable."

Under the agreement the three men hashed out, Aloys took over the Austrian business of Kupfer & Glaser as well as the Frankenreuth foundry and several associated properties, all of which were amalgamated into the firm of Aloys Kupfer, Frankenreuth. Eduard took over the remainder of E. & A. Kupfer, including the Weiden foundry, in addition to receiving a cash payment from Aloys equivalent to about $4 million. Sigmund Glaser took over the Bavarian business of Kupfer & Glaser.

In Ignaz's view, Eduard came out with the sweetest cut. "The man has kept a nice business, has actual cash, and furthermore a mortgage of about three-quarters of a million marks from Aloys," he wrote in his diary.[8] "Sigmund is to be pitied. After 25 years of trouble he really has nothing and must start all over again. He may be pleased to be finally free."

Following the breakup in April 1899, Eduard engineered a series of deals to finance the continued operations of the Weiden foundry and ensure his family's economic security. He founded *Eduard Kupfer & Söhne* with his eldest son, Heinrich, and Otto. A few days later, in concert with several other businessmen and bankers, he founded a second, publicly traded company, Glasfabrik Weiden, vorm. Ed. Kupfer AG [Weiden Glass Factory, formerly Eduard Kupfer Ltd.], with Heinrich as chairman. And a few months after that, Weiden Glass acquired Krailsheimer & Miederer, a mirror-glass maker based in Fürth.[9] The combined company, Tafel, Salin und Spiegelglas Fabriken, was initially valued at 1.7 million marks, or roughly $10 million today. Eduard, who controlled nearly 30 percent of the company's shares, was installed on the board of directors along with Heinrich, and Otto was named director of the Weiden operation.

Eduard's deal-making was likely inspired by a major shift in the way flat glass was produced that occurred around the turn of the century. The cylinder process, a labor-intensive method practiced for centuries in which workers used blowpipes to shape molten glass into hollow spheres, which were then cut and flattened, was gradually replaced by mechanized processes. Mirror glass, which requires a distortion-free surface and high transparency, was increasingly being made by the casting and rolling method, while window glass, a lower-quality product, was being produced by the so-called drawing process, which involved drawing sheets of glass directly out of the molten glass.[10] These technological advances spurred glassmakers to build new plants and modernize existing ones to remain competitive. They also led to increasing consolidation in the industry as larger, better-capitalized companies swallowed up smaller foundries.

Against this backdrop the Kupfers and other independent glassmakers faced a choice: grow larger and more efficient or shrivel and die. The merger of Weiden Glass with Krailsheimer & Miederer to form Tafel-Salin was Eduard's answer. It was a typical example of the vertical and horizontal consolidation then taking place in the Bavarian glass industry.

Aloys' share of the family business did not fare as well as Eduard's. By the time he took over the Frankenreuth *Glashütte* it was in bad shape, both financially and physically, and was operating under some questionable practices. A government inspection in October 1900 found that worker housing was inadequate, work rules were not being followed, with young men sometimes working 14- to 16-hour shifts, and the foundry itself was in serious disrepair. It didn't help matters that Aloys fell gravely ill, his sons proved to be inept businessmen, and creditors were demanding repayment of their loans.[11]

In an effort to help his ailing brother-in-law and save the business from total collapse, Eduard purchased the Frankenreuth complex in 1905 for about $1 million in today's dollars. Two months later he transferred ownership of the foundry, together with five grinding and polishing works, to Bayerische Spiegel und Spiegelglas Fabriken AG [Bavarian Mirror and Mirror Glass Factories], a publicly-traded company he co-founded with Louis and Meier Bechmann, who owned a mirror glass company in Fürth. It was Eduard's last major business deal before he died two years later at age 67.

Eduard surely died a wealthy man, but just how wealthy is not clear because he did not leave an official will. "All was regulated within the family," Dr. Müller noted, which was not unusual among Jewish families at the time.

Over the next few years the performance of the Frankenreuth foundry improved, but ultimately it was unable to compete with more modern and efficient operations. In 1926 Bayerische Spiegel closed the foundry and laid off its remaining 50 or so workers. Ten years later, the company sold the remnants of the foundry for the paltry sum of 1,500 reichsmarks – roughly equivalent to $11,000 today. One could almost hear a sigh of relief in the company's annual report: "We have been able to rid ourselves of the factory premises in Frankenreuth, which have not been required for the business for many years."

A sad postscript to the Frankenreuth story occurred in 1936, when Germany hosted the Olympics – both the Winter Games in the Bavarian Alps and the Summer Games in Berlin. In an effort to impress foreign visitors, Nazi Propaganda Minister Joseph Goebbels and Interior Minister Wilhelm Frick launched a campaign they called "*Olympia – eine Nationale Aufgabe*" [Olympics – a National Task] to spruce up the appearance of cities and towns across the country. As part of the beautification effort, the mayor of Waidhaus received a letter directing him to clean up the abandoned *Glashütte* in Frankenreuth. "Right on the Czech border directly on the main road are some factory buildings that give a distinctly poor impression and are completely derelict," the letter noted. "Please let us know at your earliest convenience how you propose to remove this nuisance and when its eradication may be expected."

After decades of slow decline, the cradle of the Kupfer glass empire was no more. In the mid-1980s, another use was found for the grounds of the old glassworks – a shooting range for a local gun club.

My grandfather Otto served as director of the Weiden factory until 1927 and was a member of the board of directors of Bayerische Spiegel until 1931. Between 1933 and 1938 he was registered with the city of Weiden as an "independent agent for oils and fats," a job title for which I could find no clear description.[12]

In 1932, Tafel-Salin, including its Weiden foundry, merged with two other German glassmakers to form Deutsche Tafelglas AG [German Plate Glass Co.], or DETAG. By that time Otto and other members of the Kupfer family were no longer involved in management, though they retained a financial stake in the company. Within a few years the Nazis would drum Jews out of every boardroom and every other corner of the German economy.

After World War II, DETAG was involved in a series of mergers, acquisitions, and name changes. In 1980 a majority stake was acquired by British-based Pilkington, the inventor of the float glass process and one of the largest flat glass manufacturers in the world. Then, in 2006, Pilkington was swallowed up by the still larger Nippon Sheet Glass Co. of Japan. The Weiden *Glasfabrik* ceased operations in 1979, at the time of my first visit to the city, but some of the factory's soot-stained brick buildings and smokestacks are still standing today.

Dad in his office, circa 1930

A BRIEF HISTORY OF ANTISEMITISM IN GERMANY

Antisemitism in Germany didn't begin with the Nazis, of course, nor did it end with them. Jews have been persecuted in Germany since at least the Middle Ages. The oppression has taken many forms, from restrictions on where they could live, whom they could marry, and which occupations they could practice to mass expulsions and bloody pogroms. Hitler, in other words, fanned the flames of a fire that had been smoldering for centuries.

The first recorded incident of Jewish persecution in Germany occurred in 1096, during the First Crusade, when peasants killed hundreds of Jews along what is now the French-German border in a series of pogroms that became known as the Rhineland Massacres. In the mid-1300s the Bubonic Plague unleashed another wave of violence against Jews, who were blamed for spreading the epidemic by poisoning wells. Thousands of Jews were killed and tens of thousands of others were violently expelled from dozens of cities.

Bavaria, predominantly Catholic and politically conservative, has a particularly violent history of antisemitism. In 1285, scores of Jews were burned alive in a Munich synagogue after being accused of committing "blood libel" – the ritual murder of Christian children to use their blood to make matzoh. A few years later some 5,000 Jews were murdered in Franconia, in northern Bavaria, in a massacre spearheaded by a knight who claimed to have received a mandate from God to exterminate the Jews. During the Bubonic Plague, Jewish residents of Wurzburg locked themselves in their houses and set them on fire rather than face the wrath of an antisemitic mob. And in 1819 anti-Jewish violence erupted again in Wurzburg before spreading to other parts of Germany. The pogroms were called the Hep Hep Riots because they were led by students chanting *Hep! Hep! Jude verrecke!* [Hep! Hep! Jew drop dead!].

In the 19th century, as Jews in Germany and other Western European countries began to gain more legal rights and greater acceptance in society, assimilation gave rise to a new wave of antisemitism. In 1849 a Bavarian government proposal to give Jews equal rights sparked widespread opposition. Hundreds of petitions were sent to the government accusing Jews of being money-hungry parasites bent on destroying Christianity.[1] One appeal from a small town near Frankfurt, signed by the mayor and the parish priest among scores of others, began this way:

Painfully and with great displeasure, we have learned of the disgrace threatening the entire Christian population of the country in that the Jews, an alien nation by origin and religion, by customs and mores, are to receive civic and political rights completely equal to those of the Bavarian people. ... We expect protection and more effective laws against Jewish swindling, against their fraud and usury, against the systematic exploitation of townspeople and countrymen who, quite commonly, after an initially small debt to the Jews, soon find themselves so ensnared that they can no longer avoid ruin.[2]

It wasn't until 1861 that restrictions on freedom of movement, choice of occupation, and ownership of land were lifted in Bavaria, allowing Jews to participate as economic equals. And it wasn't until the adoption of the Weimar Constitution in 1919, when my father was 12, that Jews and other religious minorities in Germany were fully emancipated.

After Germany's humiliating defeat in World War I, which left the economy in ruins, Jews were often made the targets of public anger and resentment. They were attacked by mobs in Munich and Berlin and the myth of Jewish ritual killings of Christian boys was revived.

Between the end of the war and Hitler's rise to power in 1933, more than 430 antisemitic associations – including one in Dad's hometown – and some 700 anti-Jewish newspapers, magazines, and periodicals were established across Germany.

Thus the stage was set for the Nazis to exploit Germany's centuries-old hatred of Jews for their own political purposes. Indeed, in the view of some historians, many Germans embraced National Socialism precisely because it offered them an outlet for their antisemitism. As Robert Runcie, the Archbishop of Canterbury, once observed: "Without centuries of Christian antisemitism, Hitler's passionate hatred would never have been so fervently echoed."

GATHERING STORM

Dad grew up during a relatively good period for German Jews. Despite the rise in antisemitic incidents following World War I, Jews were generally accepted in society and had achieved success in nearly every sector of the German economy, from law and medicine to academia and industry – the Kupfer glass business being one example.

But all that began to change in January 1933, when German President Paul von Hindenburg appointed Adolf Hitler chancellor. Almost immediately the Nazis began dismantling democratic institutions, suppressing political opposition, and orchestrating the systematic destruction of German Jewry. On April 1, the party organized a national boycott of Jewish-owned businesses. *Deutsche! Wehrt Euch! Kauft nicht bei Juden!* [Germans! Defend yourselves! Do not buy from Jews!] signs warned. A few days later came the Law for the Restoration of the Professional Civil Service, which led to the dismissal of thousands of Jews from government jobs. In May the writings of Jewish and other "un-German" authors were burned outside the Berlin Opera House.

Over the next several years more than 400 laws and decrees were issued restricting virtually every aspect of Jewish life. The so-called Nuremberg Race Laws, adopted in September 1935, prohibited marriages and extramarital sexual relations between Jews and Gentiles and declared that only people of "German blood" were eligible to be citizens. Jews were barred from serving in the military, the judiciary, and the medical profession; from using public transportation, libraries, and swimming pools; from owning cars, telephones, and radios. There were restrictions on buying real estate, precious metals, and lottery tickets. Laws mandated which hours of the day Jews could be outdoors (no later than eight in the evening in winter, nine in summer).

In August 1938 the Nazis decreed that Jews with "non-Jewish" first names must add "Israel" or "Sara" to their given names. Thus, my grandfather became Otto Israel Kupfer and his sister, Hermine Sara Klein. And then came Kristallnacht, on November 9-10, when packs of Brownshirts and other Nazi sympathizers rampaged through the streets, killing scores of Jews, burning hundreds of synagogues, and looting thousands of Jewish homes and businesses.

The Nazis had a long history in Weiden. Bavaria, after all, was the birthplace of the National Socialist German Workers' Party and the nucleus of Hitler's political power. The Fuhrer dubbed Munich, Bavaria's capital, *Hauptstadt der Bewegung* – Capital of the Movement – and Nuremberg, Bavaria's second-largest city, was the symbolic center of the Nazi regime and the traditional site of the party's bellicose annual rallies. It was also the home of *Der Stürmer* [The Attacker], a rabid antisemitic newspaper whose official slogan, displayed in large black type on the front page of each issue, was *Die Juden sind unser Unglück!* [The Jews are our misfortune!].[1]

The Weiden chapter of the NSDAP was established in 1922 by a small group that included Hans Harbauer, a businessman who became superintendent of the local unit of the SA and was later installed as mayor. In 1929 Harbauer and two other Nazis were elected to the 15-member City Council, which was then dominated by the conservative Catholic Bavarian People's Party (BVP) and the left-leaning Social Democratic Party (SPD). Although the National Socialists tried to stir up anti-Jewish sentiment, it remained a small and largely inconsequential party in town until Hitler became chancellor.

In October 1932, Hitler himself appeared at a rally in Weiden.[2] An article about his visit published in the *Oberpfälzischer Kurier*, a conservative Catholic newspaper, is notable for its undisguised disdain for the Nazi leader and his party. Although he was named chancellor a few months later, the *Kurier* suggested that the NSDAP was in serious decline – "sick at heart and in its purse" – and Hitler's decision to visit a small provincial city like Weiden was evidence that "he already considers it hopeless to attract votes in the bigger cities because his ideas can never be implemented."

The rally was held on the grounds of a local sports club. The Nazi leader was scheduled to speak at eight in the evening but didn't arrive until 11:30 p.m. He had had a busy day, stopping first in Pocking, near the Austrian border, then in Gunzenhausen, southwest of Nuremberg, and then in Nuremberg itself.

Attendees were charged a fee of two marks for the privilege of hearing the future Führer. "As much as this is to be understood in view of the known cash shortage of the Nazis," the *Kurier* sneered, "one must nonetheless really wonder how the party that claims to be a special protector of socially oppressed humanity still tries to extract a few hard-earned pennies to finance party business."

In preparation for Hitler's visit, a huge tent was erected with a capacity of 10,000 to 15,000 people, but only between 5,000 and 6,000 showed up, according to the *Kurier*. Even that number was suspect, the newspaper noted, because it included "1,500 brown-uniformed men" – a reference to the SA – and a lot of people from outside the area.

The Nazi leader spoke for half an hour "with increasing excitement," warning that President von Hindenburg "had better make room whether he wanted to or not," the *Kurier* reported. "There is nothing new to report on the content of his speech," the paper added, barely concealing a yawn. "For many it may have been an experience to hear Hitler speak. For most it was a disappointment. He was not convincing. It was much ado about nothing."

The *Kurier's* dismissive attitude toward Hitler and his party was most likely the prevailing attitude in Weiden at the time, but that began to change after he became chancellor on January 30, 1933.

Flags emblazoned with swastikas were soon fluttering from city halls across Bavaria, the Altes Rathaus in Weiden likely among them.

Over the next several months, a handful of local Jewish businessmen were arrested and sent to Dachau, a concentration camp outside Munich.[3] On April 6 the City Council was dissolved and reconstituted three weeks later with seven Nazis and eight members of the BVP. The liberal SPD was barred altogether.[4] Then in August, the BVP mayor was ousted and replaced by Harbauer, who remained in office until the end of the war.[5,6]

DAILY TORMENT

With the Nazis firmly in control of local government, life for Weiden's Jewish population became a daily torment. Jews were barred from the local swimming pool, the movie theater, and public parks. A banner was displayed at Marktplatz reading: *"Die Deutschen von Weiden können die Juden nicht leiden. Drum bleibt uns fern und habt uns gern."* [The Germans in Weiden do not like the Jews. So stay away and don't return.]. The boycott of Jewish-owned businesses intensified, and those who defied it risked having their names and photographs published in the "Shame" column of the Nazi newspaper *Bayerische Ostmark*.[1] Swastikas and slogans warning "Do not buy from Jews" and "Get out Jews" were painted on Jewish storefronts. Articles alleging Jewish malfeasance and misdeeds and letters to the editor denouncing Jews appeared regularly in the local newspapers.

It would be difficult enough to live in a society that tolerates discrimination. My friends of color know all too well what that feels like. To a lesser extent, so do my cousins in France, where attacks on Jews are commonplace. And as a gay man, I have felt the sting of homophobia many times, especially when traveling outside the protective cocoon of the San Francisco Bay Area.

But to live in a society where the government not only sanctions that discrimination but is the driving force behind it is a different order of pain. How would it feel to know that the leader of your country hates you and that the mission of his government is to destroy you? What would it be like to live in a society whose every institution – the courts, the military, the police, the schools – are in the hands of people who see no reason for you to exist?

Given Weiden's small, close-knit Jewish community, Dad and his family were no doubt aware of the arrests of local Jewish businessmen. Surely they heard about the brutal attacks on Jewish merchants, lawyers, and judges in Berlin and other German cities. And, of course, they were painfully aware of the spate of anti-Jewish decrees, boycotts, newspaper articles, signs, and so on.

What did my father think and feel as the storm clouds of antisemitism swirled around him and his family? Did his stomach flutter with anxiety every time he walked past the Rathaus? Did he shudder with fear when he went into the post office or the library? Did he tremble at the sight of a police officer or Brownshirt?

True to form, Dad never shared his feelings about that period with me, but one can get a sense of what his life was like from Michael Brenner's book, *Am Beispiel Weiden: Jüdischer Alltag im Nationalsozialismus* [The Example of Weiden: Everyday Life for Jews Under National Socialism], which is based on historical documents and interviews with survivors. Among the people Brenner interviewed were the sons of Else and Karl Steiner, a local shopkeeper, who described the terrifying night in June 1933 when the family was awakened by a pack of drunken youths shouting: "Jewish pigs." Karl was among the Jewish men who were arrested and sent to Dachau, forcing Else to close the family business, a small shop selling bedsprings, and provide for her four young children on a few marks a week in government assistance.

Walter Steiner, who attended the Jewish school in Weiden, recalled being cursed at and spit on as he walked to school, and his classmate Harry Hutzler remembered being pelted with rocks. "They would shout stuff at me like 'Jewish pig, you stink like garlic, here comes the crooked nose,' and so on. It was a daily terror," Hutzler told Brenner. "In the beginning I had a few Christian friends, but with the growing antisemitic propaganda, it was impossible for these boys to stay in touch with me. Within a year I was completely isolated." Despite attending a Jewish school, the students were expected to give the straight-armed Nazi salute when their teacher entered the classroom, Hutzler recalled, but that didn't stop them from cursing the Führer under their breath.

Another account of life in Weiden under the Nazis was written by Otto Marx, a Jewish World War I veteran and SPD member, who lived with his family in an apartment above his haberdashery.[2] On March 29, 1933, the police and SS raided his business and arrested him. He was later sent to Dachau along with two other local Jewish businessmen.[3]

Shortly after arriving at the camp Marx was ordered to report to the commandant's office. This is how he described what happened next:

I found myself in an arrest cell. Around me were four SS men each with an ox whip. They greeted me with calls of Saujude *[Jewish pig] and* Schweinhund *[pig dog], and similar insulting names. In the room was a wooden trestle and my torturers told me to lie over it. I protested strongly against this treatment [noting] that I had fought for Germany for four years in the Great War. As I raised my arms to protect myself, the notorious mass murderer Hans Steinbrenner*[4] *drew his pistol with safety catch off and put it to my temple. I could only think of my wife and child and resigned myself to my fate. They took great delight in beating me.*

Marx was assigned to work in the camp clothing store, where he could hear the screams of prisoners being beaten in their cells. Those who couldn't bear the torture any longer committed suicide, he wrote, while others were taken to the surrounding forest and shot "while trying to escape."

Marx remembered one particularly brutal night in the summer of 1934 when scores of Nazi functionaries and political opponents were beaten and shot to death. This was the Night of the Long Knives, Hitler's purge of suspected traitors within the party ranks.[5] He didn't witness the murders himself, but he was later ordered to bring sand to "soak up the blood."

After 32 months in captivity, Marx was released in December 1935 with a warning not to say a word about what he had seen or he would be sent back to Dachau and hanged. He returned to Weiden to find his hometown had changed dramatically in his absence. Jewish children were barred from attending public schools and Aryan children were required to join Hitler Youth, where they were steeped in antisemitism. When he encountered Christian acquaintances in the street, "they would slink past or greet you secretly and almost unnoticeably."

But not everyone in town was antisemitic, Marx noted, and some went out of their way to help him and his family. A few non-Jews continued to patronize his haberdashery, entering through the back door or coming after dark. On Sundays he and his family would visit Christian friends in the countryside to buy butter and beer.

Even Nazi loyalists were not all antisemites, Marx said. His dentist was a longstanding party member who continued to treat him and his family despite the prohibition against doing so. In January 1938 the dentist urged him to get out of Germany before the National Socialists' annual rally in Nuremberg in September. Fortunately for Marx, he heeded the dentist's warning. On June 15, five months before Kristallnacht, he and his family boarded a ship bound for the US.

Another first-hand account of life in Weiden under the Nazis was provided by Margot Linczyc, the granddaughter of Max Krell, the owner of a local department store. The boycott of Jewish businesses forced Krell to sell his store in 1936, leaving the family with no source of income. Linczyc was sent to live with relatives outside Berlin, where she survived the war by becoming a so-called U-boat person, hiding in the shadows of the underground. She managed to escape to Switzerland in 1943 on a train packed with German troops. "They deprived us step by step," Linczyc recalled.[6] "We were so numbed that we just automatically did everything we were told."

The best-known account of everyday life under the Nazis was written by Victor Klemperer, a Jewish professor of Romance languages in Dresden, capital of the neighboring state of Saxony.[7] *I Will Bear Witness: A Diary of the Nazi Years* paints a chilling picture of Klemperer's comfortable, middle-class life slowly but inexorably unraveling.[8] Although he was married to a Christian woman and had converted to Protestantism, that didn't spare him the Nazis' wrath. His teaching hours were cut back, and eventually he lost his job. He was forced to give up his car, his telephone, even his typewriter. Cigarettes became a luxury he could no longer afford. He was even forced to euthanize his beloved cat Muschel because Jews were no longer allowed to own pets.

From the moment the Nazis took power, Klemperer wrote, he had a sense of a "swiftly approaching catastrophe." He and his wife felt increasingly isolated as Jewish friends and colleagues were arrested or fled the country, and those who remained were too frightened to speak out. They talked politics in whispers, with the windows closed. Pictures of Hitler were everywhere, in newspapers and posters, at the pharmacy and the grocery store.

Some of the indignities Klemperer was subjected to were almost ludicrous in their pettiness. Local officials inspected his garden and, finding too many weeds, ordered him to hire a gardener to remove them. The only pleasures left to him and his wife were having coffee with friends and going to the movies, but even there they could not escape the Nazi propaganda machine: newsreels were filled with the Third Reich's self-adulation and triumphalism, with images of rapturous receptions for Hitler and boastful speeches by Goebbels.

"I am no longer going to worry about what happens after tomorrow," he wrote on June 28, 1937. "It's all so pointless."

Four days earlier, on June 24, my father submitted an application to the US consulate in Stuttgart for a visa to immigrate to the United States. His sponsor was Siegfried Herrmann, his grandmother Therese's youngest brother, who had immigrated to the America as a teenager half a century earlier. On October 14, Dad officially notified the city of Cham that he intended to immigrate to the US. The next day he crossed the border into France. He never stepped foot in Germany again.

As more and more Jewish families fled Germany, the regional

Nazi paper *Bayerische Ostmark* published a brief notice in May 1938 trumpeting the decline in Weiden's Jewish population:[9]

For the first time since the turn of the century, the number of Jews living in Weiden is below 100. We hope that these as well will make up their minds to leave. Weiden is lucky to have lost half of the Jewish bloodsuckers since 1933. We would consider ourselves even more lucky if the last Jew would shake the dust of our hometown off his feet. The hometown that he has plundered. We definitely would not shed any tears for him.

KRISTALLNACHT AND BEYOND

A year after my father immigrated to the United States, the growing hostility toward Jews in Germany reached a bloody crescendo on the night of November 9, 1938, when mobs of SA and other Nazi partisans rampaged through the streets, attacking Jewish homes, businesses, and religious sites. By the time it was over, at least 91 Jews were killed,[1] some 30,000 Jewish men were rounded up and sent to concentration camps, about 7,500 Jewish businesses were vandalized and looted, nearly 1,000 synagogues were sent up in flames, and countless Jewish homes, hospitals, schools, and cemeteries were damaged or destroyed. In many cities, police and firefighters stood by and watched as the devastation unfolded. Adding insult to grievous injury, the Nazis imposed a fine of 1 billion reichsmarks – equivalent to about $400 million today – on the German Jewish community and confiscated all insurance payouts to Jews whose businesses and homes were damaged.

The Nazis claimed the violence was a spontaneous reaction to the killing of a German Embassy official in Paris by Polish Jewish teenager whose family had been expelled from Germany. But there is little doubt that the assassination was a pretext and that the pogrom was planned to coincide with the 15th anniversary of the so-called

Beer Hall Putsch, Hitler's failed attempt to overthrow the Bavarian government.[2]

The violence in Weiden began after a rally in the nearby town of Neustadt to mark the 1923 Munich uprising, according to a study published by a local historical society.[3] Shortly after the celebration ended at 9:45 p.m., Kreisleiter Franz Bacherl, the top Nazi official for the Weiden district, received a call from the office of his superior in Bayreuth, Gauleiter Fritz Wächtler, directing him to "rattle" the Jewish community. Bacherl, a former schoolteacher, ordered local SA members to report in civilian clothes to the Rathaus. From there they were dispatched to three primary targets: Jewish homes and businesses, the synagogue, and the home and office of Dr. Franz Josef Pfleger, a Catholic lawyer and outspoken critic of Hitler's policies whose clientele included many Jews. The police, meanwhile, were ordered by Mayor Harbauer to begin taking male Jews into "protective custody."

The city's Jewish families were rousted from their beds and herded to the Rathaus, some still in their nightclothes despite the chilly November weather. Many arrived bloodied and injured after being beaten by their captors. Their homes, meanwhile, were vandalized and looted.

An SA man was dispatched to stand guard outside the Kupfer villa at 33 Max-Regerstrasse. He was later joined by a handful of others dressed in civilian clothes who smashed the villa's leaded windows and broke into the house. Otto, 65, and his sister Mina, 68, were arrested and taken to City Hall.

Shortly after 2 a.m. a rabble of Brownshirts stormed the synagogue, overturning furniture and smashing windows and lights. They dragged the Torah and other religious objects into the street and set them on fire. Silver pieces, carpets, and other valuables, including the temple's poverty fund, were looted. The building itself was spared from total destruction only because it was located on a block of attached buildings and Harbauer feared that if it were set on fire the flames would spread to the adjoining homes and businesses.

Around the same time a group of men broke into the home of

merchant Joseph Wilmersdörfer, dragged him and his 62-year-old wife out of the closet where they had been hiding, and beat them. The couple were brought to the Rathaus but were later released because the police apparently didn't have a proper arrest warrant. They returned to find their house in shambles, with windows broken, furniture toppled, and mirrors, lamps, and dishes shattered. Meanwhile, another group attacked the home of Leopold Engelmann, a wealthy Jewish cattle dealer, who was beaten with a club and ridiculed as a *Judensau* while his house was ransacked.

Sometime after 3 a.m. a mob of about 50 people battered down the front door of Dr. Pfleger's house and rampaged through the living quarters and office, smashing furniture, splattering raw eggs on the walls, spraying ink on the beds, and shredding the lawyer's files and books. Pfleger and his son managed to save themselves by hiding in the attic.

By 6 a.m. nearly every Jew in Weiden had been arrested and the city center was strewn with scraps of paper and shards of glass.[4] Otto and Mina, along with other elderly men, women, and children, were later released, but 23 Jewish men were taken to the local jail before being shipped to Dachau.

Otto and Mina's brother Moritz, who lived in Wiesbaden, a spa town west of Frankfurt, suffered a similar fate. He was held in Dachau for 10 days before being released. Four years later, on September 19, 1942, a month after Otto and Mina were deported to Theresienstadt, Moritz was arrested and sent to Mauthausen, a concentration camp in northern Austria, where he died five days later.

The pogrom in Weiden was spearheaded by the local SA, but the Brownshirts had plenty of help. Michael Brenner wrote about a Jewish high school student named Hermann Haussmann who recalled that his own teacher was among the people who had raided his family's house. The next day in school the teacher bragged about his role in the attack and mocked Haussmann for crying out for help. "We showed the Jews who's the boss last night," the teacher boasted, according to Haussmann. "Manni was really scared. He screamed for help the entire time." Another witness reported seeing a pack of teenage girls beating Jewish women and girls on the street.

After Kristallnacht, the Nazi policy of *Arisierung* took a more aggressive turn. Rather than relying on harassment and intimidation to force Jews to close or sell their businesses, the government began confiscating their property. Those who refused to cooperate were thrown into jail.

By then Dad's family was no longer involved in the glass industry. The exact circumstances are not clear, but it was most likely the result of continuing consolidation in the industry combined with the growing suppression of Jewish-owned businesses.

Before the Nazis came to power, Jews owned about 100,000 businesses in Germany, including factories, professional practices, book and newspaper publishers, and some 50,000 stores. By 1938, the majority of those businesses no longer existed and only 9,000 stores remained. The most prized properties and businesses often ended up in the hands of high-ranking party officials.

In March 1939, four months after Kristallnacht, my grandfather and his family were forced to sell the Kupfer villa. The house, which was considered one of the most desirable properties in town, became the object of a heated tug of war between Mayor Harbauer, who wanted to seize it for the city, and Bartholomäus Wies, a next-door neighbor who owned a local transportation company.[5]

In an effort to sway Nazi authorities in Bayreuth, who had jurisdiction over the sale, Harbauer accused Wies and his family of being regular churchgoers – apparently a cardinal sin in the Nazi mayor's view. Even worse, according to Harbauer, Wies had the audacity to be "friendly" with Jews. As a case in point, the mayor noted that Wies had agreed to allow Otto and Mina to continue living in the villa after the property had been sold, presumably to give them time to find another place to live.[6,7]

Fritz Wächtler, the Nazi *Gauleiter*, was apparently unimpressed with Harbauer's arguments and approved the sale of the villa to Wies for 45,000 reichsmarks, or about $335,000 in today's dollars. But there was a catch: Wies had to agree to lease the house to the National Socialists for their regional headquarters. Typical of forced sales of Jewish properties under *Arisierung,* the sale price was significantly below market value. After the war, a restitution lawsuit filed by my father and his brother determined that the property had been worth 60,000-70,000 RM, or roughly $450,000 today.

Harbauer denounced the decision to sell the villa to Wies as "a display of malicious obstinacy against Weiden and its mayor."[8] He proposed that the villa be used instead to house the city's remaining Jewish population, which by then had dwindled to fewer than 75, but Nazi officials rejected that idea.

By the time Otto and Mina were forced to sell the villa they were in serious financial straits and what money they had left was difficult to access because of government restrictions on Jewish bank accounts. Moreover, proceeds from the sale of the house – even if they could get their hands on it – would have to be divided with their seven other surviving siblings, who were joint owners of the property.

According to files in the Hessen State Archive, an application submitted in June 1939 to the Foreign Exchange Office in Nuremberg on the family's behalf pleaded with the authorities to release the funds: "All these [Kupfer] brothers and sisters without exception are without funds and need money to maintain themselves and to prepare for immigration."[9] Two months later, Otto sent a letter to the Custom Office in Nuremberg stating that the impounded money was "urgently required" for living expenses and immigration purposes.[10] And the following week, in an appeal to the Foreign Exchange Office in Frankfurt, he wrote: "I humbly wish to inform you that I possess no assets whatsoever. All I have is the proceeds of the sale of the house in Weiden, which I have to share with eight brothers and sisters."[11]

Another file in the Hessen State Archive reveals the lengths to which the Nazis went to prevent Jews from moving their assets out of Germany.[12] The Gestapo had apparently launched a criminal investigation of Otto, Mina, and a local businessman named Kohnmünch. Their crime? The Kupfers had purchased candy at Kohnmünch's store to send to relatives abroad, including my father in the US. The secret police learned about this grave offense from an informant at the post office who had noticed that the packages were addressed to people "with obvious Jewish names."

The case file includes transcripts of an interview the Gestapo conducted with Kohnmünch in May 1939, and subsequent interviews with Otto and Mina. In his statement, my grandfather acknowledged that he had purchased the candy but said he hadn't realized it was against the law to send it abroad. "I sent these packages to my children and nieces because I couldn't send them anything else," he explained.

Mina confessed that she had asked her brother to send candy to her daughter Rosl in London. The cost of the illicit gift was two reichsmarks, or about $1.20. She also admitted sending Rosl a pair of stockings and a flashlight, which together cost about $1.

It's not clear how the candy investigation ended or whether the packages were ever delivered. Perhaps the informant ate the evidence.

Otto and Mina continued living in the villa for several months after it was sold, before moving to Frankfurt. It's not clear whether they were forced to move there or did so voluntarily, but by that time large cities were considered safer havens for Jews because it was easier for them to blend in. Frankfurt was also closer to their brother Moritz in Wiesbaden.

As Nazi persecution intensified and landlords were pressured to evict Jewish tenants, Otto and Mina were forced to move several times in Frankfurt. Their last known address was Eschersheimer Landstrasse 39, an apartment house where Jewish families were forced to live before being deported. They were living in this so-called *Judenhaus* when they were rounded up by the Gestapo on August 18, 1942.

In April 2022, during an unexpected layover in Frankfurt, I took the S-Bahn from the airport into the city and walked to Eschersheimer Landstrasse 39. I found an elegant but slightly dilapidated five-story building on a main street near the city center.

The ground floor, partially obscured by scaffolding, was occupied by a store selling pianos and other musical instruments. The apartment house was attached to a modern building occupied by the Frankfurt University of Music and Performing Arts, a state school for music, theater, and dance, which had apparently taken over the upper floors of the adjoining building.[13]

It was dark by the time I found the apartment house. As I stood outside imagining my grandfather and his sister being carted off by the Gestapo a night watchman approached me and muttered something I couldn't understand. I snapped a few pictures with my phone and headed back to the airport.

In 1983, nearly 40 years after the fall of the Third Reich, the Weiden newspaper *Oberpfälzer Nachrichten* published a controversial five-part series about the local Nazi party titled "*Weiden 1933: Eine Stadt Wird Braun*" [Weiden 1933: A City Goes Brown]. Written by Bernhard M. Baron, an SPD member and former head of the city's office of culture and tourism, and historian Karl Bayer, the article identified local residents who had been prominent members of the SS. The most notorious was Martin Gottfried Weiss, a former commandant at Dachau who was arrested after the war and hanged for war crimes. Baron told me the article caused quite a stir in town when it was published and that he and Bayer became the target of verbal attacks by the families of the SS men they identified.

The local Nazi-controlled government treated the Jewish population "with incredible brutality and cruelty," Baron and Bayer wrote. Contrary to what many people told me during my visits to Weiden, the persecution of Jews was common knowledge in town. The arrests and deportations were generally reported in the local newspapers, and local authorities kept meticulous records of their efforts to "dejudify" the city.

In 1932, the year before Hitler came to power, there were 171 Jews living in Weiden, according to city records. Five years later, in 1937, the year my father fled to the US, that number had declined to 105. By May 1939, six months after Kristallnacht, there were 57 Jews left, including Otto and Mina, who moved to Frankfurt the following month. By July there were 28 and by October, shortly after Germany invaded Poland, there were only 16.

On April 4, 1942, nine Jews from Weiden were deported to Trawniki, a concentration camp outside Lublin, in eastern Poland; none survived. The last three Jews officially registered as residents of Weiden were sent to a home for elderly Jews in Regensburg on May 27, 1942. From there they were deported to Theresienstadt on September 23, about a month after Otto and Mina were sent there, where they suffered the same fate. One Jewish woman, Rosa Hoffmann, who was married to a Protestant doctor, survived the war by hiding in an unknown location in Weiden, according to city historian Sebastian Schott. She was liberated by the Americans in April 1945.

Of the 168 Jews living in Weiden in June 1933, five months after the Nazis took power, 88 emigrated to other countries, including 20 to the UK; 17 (including my father) to the US; 14 to Palestine; 11 to Czechoslovakia; seven (including my father's brother, Ernst) to France; five to Argentina; four to Cuba; and several others to Kenya and Uruguay. Fifty-four moved to other, mostly larger cities in Germany. Many, if not all, of these people, like my grandfather and his sister, were eventually murdered in concentration camps. Only two Jewish residents returned to the city after the war – Lothar Friedmann, the shopkeeper I met during my first visit to Weiden, and Justin Spitz, the owner of a local cinema, who emigrated to Palestine in 1933 and returned in 1947. All told, about one-third of the city's Jewish population died in the Shoah, about the same proportion as in Germany as a whole.

Of Eduard and Fanni's 10 children who survived into adulthood, eight, including Otto and Mina, died in concentration camps or Jewish ghettos, and Nazi persecution no doubt contributed to the death of a ninth. (Berta died of malnutrition in 1941, at age 73, after she and her husband, Dr. Ferdinand Herrmann, were forced to move out of their Vienna apartment and no doubt feared arrest and deportation at any moment.) The 10th child, Heinrich, Otto's eldest brother, died of natural causes long before the war.

Including aunts, uncles, and first cousins, 16 members of my father's family were murdered by the Nazis.

OTTO'S CHOICE

When I tell people that my grandfather died in a Nazi concentration camp after my father fled to the United States, the question I often get is, why did he decide to stay behind? Why didn't he escape with my father when he had the chance?

I don't know the answer to that question but it's not difficult to imagine what it might be. First of all, my grandfather was nearly 60 when Hitler came to power, an age when (as I can attest) a certain inertia sets in and the prospect of uprooting oneself and starting a new life in a foreign country would be daunting. Other than his younger son and a few distant relatives, he knew virtually no one in the US. And unlike Dad, who had studied English in school and had at least a rudimentary command of the language, my grandfather spoke little or no English. His efforts to learn, after my father emigrated, were fraught with frustration. ("I just can't get it into my head," he lamented to Dad in a letter in April 1941.)

Immigrating to the United States also would have meant a big financial sacrifice. Restrictions on what Jews were allowed to take out of Germany would have forced him to forfeit almost all his property and other assets.

In the early years of the Nazi regime, the official government policy was to encourage Jewish emigration as a means of achieving its goal of *Judenrein* [cleansed of Jews]. But by the time Dad immigrated to the US in the fall of 1937, the gates were beginning to close, and in January 1942, with the adoption of The Final Solution, they were slammed shut.

To make matters worse, the United States did not exactly roll out the red carpet for Jewish refugees. Then, as now, Washington imposed strict quotas on the number of people who could immigrate from a given country. In 1939, for example, 27,370 US visas were issued to German nationals – less than 10 percent of the number that had applied for one.[1] Applicants were forced to navigate a complicated process that required them to submit identity papers, police and medical certificates, exit and transit permissions, and a financial affidavit, among other documents.

And it wasn't as if America was the garden of Eden in those days. The US in the mid-1930s was still in the grip of the Great Depression, with unemployment ranging from nearly 25 percent in 1933 to over 14 percent in 1937. Otto knew that Robert was struggling to make a living in Connecticut, working in a series of low-paying jobs. If his 30-year-old English-speaking son were floundering in his adopted country, how would someone twice his age who didn't speak the language fare?

Naturally, if my grandfather had known in October 1937 how bad things would get, he would have left with my father. Had he known that a year later Nazi storm troopers would rampage through the streets of Weiden, smashing the windows of Jewish businesses, sacking the synagogue, and rounding up every Jew in town, he would have left. Had he known that he would be forced to sell his house and surrender most of his possessions, that he would be barred from eating in restaurants or going to the public library, that he would be prohibited from sitting on a park bench or walking the streets at certain hours, he would have left. And, of course, had he known that he and millions of other Jews would be murdered in concentration camps.

But in the fall of 1937, he knew none of that. What he did know was that he was a man approaching old age who had lived almost his entire life in a small corner of Bavaria.[2] He knew that his family had run a successful glassmaking business for generations, a business that had once employed hundreds of workers, and had been respected members of their community. And he knew that, until recently, he had lived a life of privilege, replete with big cars, horses and stables, and vacations at posh resorts.

Like so many other German Jews at the time, Otto no doubt clung to the hope that things would get better, or at least that they wouldn't get any worse. In a modern, industrialized nation like Germany, they told themselves, decency and civility would win out in the end. Sooner or later the German people would come to their senses and toss Hitler and his odious henchmen out of power. Sooner or later the Nazi nightmare would end and life would return to normal.

And who could imagine the magnitude of the evil perpetrated by the Nazis? Even now, more than half a century later, it is difficult to grasp.

Hindsight, of course, is 20-20. If someone had told my grandfather in the fall of 1937: you can go now but you must leave behind all your money, property, and other possessions or you can stay while your world slowly disintegrates and, in a few years, you will die an agonizing death in a fetid swamp in western Czechoslovakia, the choice would have been clear. But that wasn't the choice. By the time my grandfather and millions of other German Jews realized what the endgame was, it was too late. The escape hatches were sealed.

A RETIREMENT HOME IN BOHEMIA

On Tuesday, August 18, 1942, sometime between four and five in the afternoon, Train Da 503 – designated Transport XII/1 by the Gestapo – pulled away from Platform 40 on the eastern wing of Frankfurt's Grossmarkthalle. Its destination was a small town north of Prague called Bohusovice. The train was packed with more than 1,000 passengers. Among them were my grandfather Otto, identified as prisoner No. 443, and his sister Mina, prisoner No. 417.[1] Both would be dead by the end of the year.

I found this information in the archives of Yad Vashem and the US Holocaust Memorial Museum. Other details were gleaned from histories of the Holocaust and of Theresienstadt in particular. The Nazis were known to be meticulous recordkeepers, but it still amazes me that they recorded their evil deeds in such detail. Did they feel no guilt or shame? Did they not fear the judgment of history? Of God? Apparently, any such concerns were outweighed by the imperative to rid the Fatherland of Jews.

If Dad knew the specifics of his father's death, he never shared them with me. My grandfather died in a Nazi concentration camp, that's all he told me. When or how he learned about Otto's death, I don't know. In many cases families of Holocaust victims did not receive official notification for months or years after the war, if ever.

My grandfather's deportation and murder was the result of a carefully conceived and methodically executed plan called the *Endlösung der Judenfrage* [Final Solution to the Jewish Question]. It was set in motion on January 20, 1942, at a meeting of senior Nazi officials in a villa outside Berlin, where it was announced that Hitler had approved the "evacuation" of all European Jews to the East. Evacuation, of course, was Nazi code for extermination.

The plan, in essence, was this: round up every Jew they could get their hands on, deport them to German-occupied Poland, Belorussia, or the Baltic States, and kill them. To avoid legal or political complications, the Nazis decided to make a few exceptions: Jews married to non-Jews, though persecuted, were generally not deported.[2] In addition, Jews who were over 65, disabled war veterans, recipients of the Iron Cross, or those considered to be of "special merit," such as artists, musicians, and other prominent figures whose disappearance might arouse suspicion, would be sent to a Jewish ghetto in Bohemia called Theresienstadt, the German name for the old fortress town of Terezín.

On May 15, 1942, Gestapo Chief Heinrich Müller issued orders to begin the deportations to Theresienstadt. Residents of Jewish old age homes and other elderly Jews were designated as the first group to go. The Germans even had a special name for the trains that would carry them – *Altertransporte,* or transports for the elderly. In August and September, the Gestapo organized three large transports from Frankfurt with a total of 3,501 passengers. Otto and Mina were on the first.

To encourage their victims' cooperation, the Nazis portrayed Theresienstadt as a pleasant spa town with villas overlooking a park, well-tended gardens, and healing mineral baths. It was a cruel but credible deception because Bohemia was known for its natural beauty and swanky resorts. Dad's photo album contains a number of pictures of him with his father and girlfriend Lotte in Karlsbad, the storied spa town set in the pine-clad hills of western Bohemia.

The roundup for Transport XII/1 began on Sunday afternoon, August 16. Otto, Mina, and the other residents of the *Judenhaus* were allowed to bring a single suitcase. Although it was summertime, when daytime temperatures in Frankfurt typically reached the mid-70s, they dressed in layers so they could bring as many clothes as possible. Many wore heavy overcoats in preparation for the harsh Bohemian winters.

Before leaving, the victims were required to sign phony home purchase agreements, or *Heimeinkaufsverträge,* which promised lifelong accommodation, food, and medical care in exchange for deposits of up to 80,000 reichsmarks (roughly equivalent to $500,000 today). The deposits were calculated based on each person's age and ability to pay. The money was turned over to the Gestapo and eventually made its way to the Reich Main Security Office, or RSHA, the organization overseeing the deportations. So, in effect, the victims were made to finance their own murders.

Tilly Cahn, the Gentile wife of a Jewish lawyer, summed up the situation in her diary:

All their property has been transferred to the Reichsvereinigung der Juden in Deutschland [Reich's Association of Jews in Germany, a Jewish umbrella group]. *But behind this institution stands the Gestapo which is eager to lay its hands on property that until now the state had been looting via the Ministry of Finance. We were told, of course, that this money will be used for our sustenance in Theresienstadt. But for how long? The money is running out with each passing day. It's shocking how calm and optimistic the deportees are ...* [3]

The elderly Jews were led out, loaded onto trucks or carts, and driven to one of two assembly areas. Other members of the Jewish community provided assistance, moving the deportees' luggage to the collection points and helping them fill out the paperwork required by the Gestapo.

This is how Cahn described the scene:

A heart-rending tragedy – all the elderly, nearly all in poor health, wearing three layers of clothing, a suitcase, a bag of food in hand. On Sunday afternoon from 16:00 onward, the people were placed aboard trucks or carts, one after another. Some were taken to the collection point on Hermesweg and some to the one on Rechneigrabenstrasse with their luggage ... where they spent two nights in severe overcrowded conditions on mattresses. The transport was carried out by Gestapo headquarters. We were not allowed to visit them anymore ... [4]

Grossmarkthalle, the wholesale market, was a convenient debarkation point because the cavernous warehouse was linked by a rail spur to the Ostbahnhof, Frankfurt's eastern train station. So the deportees could be herded directly onto the train from the platform that ran alongside the market.

Cahn recorded the moment Transport XXI/1 departed: "Now it is Tuesday, August 18, between 17:00-18:00, and the train appears to be departing for Theresienstadt. I feel terrible; this feeling will not leave me. The transport also includes very ill people ... from the hospital."[5]

In some respects, the passengers on Transport XXI/1 were more fortunate than other deportees. They rode in passenger carriages, which presumably had proper seats, ventilation, and sanitary facilities, rather than the cattle cars that were later used to ship millions of Jews to their deaths. They were not kicked and clubbed by SS guards or forced to huddle on the floor, sometimes one on top of the other, for hours or days, with no food or water and nothing but a bucket to relieve themselves.[6]

Traveling through the night, the *Altertransport* headed north to Fulda, then east to Dresden, before turning south and crossing the border into Czechoslovakia. Perhaps Otto and Mina had each other to provide a modicum of warmth and comfort during what must have been an agonizing journey, but it's just as likely they were separated in all the confusion surrounding the deportation and forced to confront their fate alone.

What was going through my grandfather's head as the train rumbled through the beech-clad hills of the Hessen countryside? Did he think about his long dead wife and parents? Did he hold out any hope of seeing his sons Robert and Ernst again or meeting his granddaughter Monique, born nine months earlier in France?[7] Did he long for the calm and comfort of the Kupfer villa? Or was he already beyond hope, beyond feeling? After years of being stripped of one right after another, after losing his home, his children, his work, was there anything left to think or feel? Or was he already resigned to death, perhaps even wishing for it?

In W. G. Sebald's novel *Austerlitz,* the title character paints a haunting portrait of Theresienstadt based on an account written by a survivor.[8] Austerlitz depicts detainees arriving at the camp "already ravaged in body and spirit, no longer in their right minds, delirious, frequently unable to remember their own names." Those who survived the brutal deportation process often suffered "extreme psychopathic personality changes ... which generally resulted in a kind of infantilism divorcing them from reality and entailing an almost total loss of the ability to speak and act."

Transport XII/1 rolled into Bohusovice on Wednesday, August 19. If my grandfather and the other passengers had any illusions about what awaited them, they were quickly dispelled. The deportees were greeted by a phalanx of SS guards armed with machine guns and green-uniformed Czech gendarmes. Exhausted, hungry, and dazed, they were marched with their luggage two miles to the gates of the ghetto. Those who were too old or weak to walk were loaded onto trucks or platforms towed by tractors. In the distance loomed the gray walls of the old fortress town and the blue-tinged mountains of Bohemia.

In his diary, Gonda Redlich, a 23-year-old teacher from Prague who was deported to Theresienstadt in December 1941, described the scene after the transport carrying my grandfather and his sister arrived:[9]

Very hot. Yesterday, they stripped the clothes from women that came from Germany and checked them naked. Maybe they wanted to find gold or silver. They thoroughly checked the transport which will leave the ghetto, until few retained anything but the clothes on their backs.[10]

The new arrivals were herded into a dank subterranean depot called the *Schleuse* [sluice], where they languished for hours, sometimes days, while their captors painstakingly filled out paperwork and inspected their bags. Items on an official list of contraband – money, jewelry, and other valuables, as well as clothing, linens, soap, toilet paper, and tobacco – were confiscated and either distributed to camp personnel or sent back to Germany. Less desirable items ended up in shops where the prisoners were, in effect, permitted to buy them back with special ghetto money issued by the SS. The captives were then herded into one of several dark, crowded barracks.[11]

Among the more than 1,000 passengers on Transport XII/1 were half a dozen children under the age of 13 and 54 people over 85. By the time the train arrived in Bohusovice, 11 passengers had already died. Within two years, more than half of the deportees succumbed to malnutrition or disease and nearly one-third of the others were sent to Auschwitz, Treblinka, or another death camp.[12] Only 17 survived the war.

My grandfather died on December 27 – 130 days after arriving at Theresienstadt. According to a death certificate provided by Czech authorities, he died at 12:40 p.m. in the Surgical Department of the General Hospital – Room 37 to be precise, as the SS officials who administered the camp were wont to be. The cause of death was recorded as "cellulitis of left hand and lower arm. Condition after amputation." So it appears he died from a bacterial infection after part of his body – a single finger? an entire hand? – was amputated.

On September 26, five weeks after arriving in Theresienstadt, Mina was shipped to Treblinka, northeast of Warsaw. I never found a death certificate but, like most of the roughly 900,000 Jews murdered there, she was most likely sent to the gas chambers immediately after arriving.

Someone once told me – I think it was my cousin Erich, but I'm not sure – that Otto had died after cutting his hand on a barbed wire fence while trying to grab a potato. I don't know if the story is true, but the image of my grandfather reaching through a fence to steal a potato still haunts me.

From the Nazis' point of view, Theresienstadt was an ideal location for a Jewish ghetto. Set at the marshy confluence of the Eger and Elbe rivers, it was originally built in the late 1700s by Austrian Emperor Joseph II as a fortress.[13] It consisted of a fortified town to the west of the Eger protected by a double set of brick walls with a moat running between them and a smaller fortress to the east, also protected by brick walls and a moat.

The complex took 10 years to build and when it was completed, in 1790, it was regarded as all but impregnable. But it was never used in battle and its fortifications gradually grew obsolete. By the end of the 19th century the walled town had been turned into a garrison and the Small Fortress was used to hold military and political prisoners. Its most infamous prisoner was a teenage anarchist from Serbia named Gavrilo Princip who assassinated Archduke Franz Ferdinand, the heir to the Austro-Hungarian Empire, the incident that sparked World War I.

Theresienstadt served several purposes for the Germans. First, it was a ghetto and labor camp for the elderly, disabled war veterans, and other Jews of "special merit." Second, it was a transit camp, a way station for Jews, like Mina, who were later dispatched to Treblinka, Auschwitz, or other death camps in eastern Europe. Third, and perhaps most important, it was a "model settlement" designed to deceive the world about the true nature of the Nazis' genocidal deportation program.

To prop up the fiction that Theresienstadt was a spa town where elderly Jews could retire in safety and dignity, the Nazis furnished the ghetto with a post office, a lending library, shops, and a café. There was even a court where petty crimes were adjudicated. A postage stamp was issued depicting the ghetto as a rural idyll, with a stream winding through a wooded meadow and mountains and billowy clouds in the distance.

The first Jews to arrive in Theresienstadt were deported from Bohemia and Moravia in November 1941. Later they came from Germany, Austria, Denmark, the Netherlands, and other western European countries. They were for the most part middle class and educated – industrialists and bank managers, lawyers, doctors, rabbis, and university professors, writers, artists, and musicians.

Terezín had about 8,000 inhabitants before the war, but under the Nazis the population swelled to more than 60,000 at times. The prisoners were housed in military barracks, with 60 or 70 people packed into rooms designed to hold 10 soldiers. There were no beds;

the more fortunate slept shoulder-to-shoulder in lofts, others made do on the floor or in casemates. Nor was there any heat; the prisoners burned bags of sawdust to stave off the cold. They ate their meager rations – watery potato soup, bread, and coffee – in the barracks because there were no mess halls. They did their washing and laundry at a water pump in the courtyard and relieved themselves in open trenches.

A young Berliner named Arthur Karl Heinz Oertelt, who was deported to Theresienstadt in March of 1943 with his mother and brother, described his experience in chilling detail in a diary discovered after the war:

... We soon became infested with lice, fleas, and bedbugs. We became obsessed with thoughts of food. Our soup was dished out from a huge barrel by lazy men who didn't bother to stir it, leaving the good food chunks near the bottom. I had to time myself just right. If I was at the front of the line, I'd get mostly the watery parts. If I was too far back, I might get nothing at all or watery soup from the top of a newly arrived barrel.[14]

Heinz and his brother survived the war, but their mother died in Auschwitz.

Although Theresienstadt had no gas chambers or other mechanisms of mass murder, the death rate was high. This, too, was by design, the inevitable result of the advanced age of many of the prisoners combined with the overcrowded conditions, inadequate sanitary facilities, malnutrition, and prevalence of infectious diseases such as diphtheria, scarlet fever, and typhus. Between 100 and 150 prisoners died on a typical day.[15]

The death rate was particularly high in the Small Fortress, where prisoners were subjected to extraordinary cruelty. During the war, it was primarily used to hold communists, anti-Fascist guerrillas, and other partisans, but many Jews were confined there as well for joining the resistance or breaking the rules of the ghetto. Prisoners accused of the most serious violations were held, often naked, in windowless solitary cells. Scores of prisoners were tortured and executed in an adjoining prison yard, near an archway painted with the infamous Nazi slogan *Arbeit Macht Frei* and buried in mass graves in the surrounding woods. The most feared guard at the Small Fortress was an Austrian named Stephan Rojko, nicknamed "the butcher of Theresienstadt" because of his wanton brutality. Rojko, who referred to prisoners as "pieces," was known to collect the gold teeth of his victims and keep them in a glass jar on his desk.

The critically ill were placed in a makeshift hospital ward where fellow prisoners tended to them as best they could. There was no shortage of doctors, surgeons, and nurses among the captives, but their efforts were hampered by primitive equipment and meager supplies. Those who suffered from extreme mental conditions were confined to the Cavalier Barracks, which served as a psychiatric ward. Most patients there died within a week.

At first the dead were buried in individual graves in a large field behind the camp store, but as the death toll rose the bodies were dumped in mass graves or incinerated in the crematorium, where four naphtha-powered furnaces raged day and night, consuming up to 200 bodies a day. At times more than 500 bodies were stacked up in the central morgue waiting to be disposed of. The ashes from the crematorium were stored in huge underground urns. Toward the end of the war, as the Red Army closed in, the SS dumped the remains into the Eger in an effort to conceal its horrific handiwork.

Theresienstadt was organized and run with typical Nazi efficiency. Every function and responsibility was delineated and regulated with fanatical zeal. Able-bodied prisoners were required to work at menial, often grueling jobs ranging from making cardboard boxes, mending clothes, and shearing rabbits to building coffins, digging graves, and pushing carts piled with corpses through the crowded ghetto streets to the crematorium.

Obsessed with numerical accuracy, the SS counted the population of Theresienstadt on a regular basis. *Austerlitz* describes one census, on a cold, wet day in November 1943, when the entire population of the ghetto, more than 40,000 people – including children, the elderly, and the sick – were roused at dawn and marched outside the gates of the town to a fog-shrouded field. They were forced to stand for hours in block formations behind numbered wooden boards. Finally, around three in the afternoon, a group of SS men arrived on motorbikes to count heads. They repeated the tally twice to make sure it was accurate. Then they rode off, without bothering to dismiss the wretched assembly.

This is how *Austerlitz* described the scene:

... this great crowd of many thousands stood out in the Bohusevice basin on that grey 10th of November drenched to the skin and increasingly distressed until well after dark, bowed and swaying like reeds in the showers that now swept over the countryside, before finally, driven to it by a wave of panic, they poured back into the town ... .

Some 300 prisoners died of hypothermia over the next several days.

As in other ghettos, the Nazis set up a Council of Jewish Elders that nominally governed the settlement but was in fact a mechanism to pacify and control the population. Members of the council were given the grim task of deciding which residents to deport to the death camps. Most of them suffered the same fate themselves, and the few who survived were later vilified as collaborators.

Despite the abysmal living conditions and the constant threat of being sent to an extermination camp, residents of Theresienstadt managed to create a remarkably rich cultural life. They wrote and staged plays, composed songs and performed concerts, wrote and recited poetry, made art and delivered lectures on subjects ranging from history to economics and medicine.

In late 1943 – a year after my grandfather's death – as reports about Nazi death camps began to emerge, the International Red Cross asked the German government for permission to inspect Theresienstadt. Seizing on the visit as an opportunity to present the ghetto as a model settlement, the Germans launched an ambitious *Verschönerungsaktion,* or beautification campaign. A circus tent that had been erected in the town square to house the box factory was dismantled and replaced with fresh plantings, park benches, and signposts painted with floral designs. The café was furnished with outdoor tables and umbrellas so residents could enjoy a cup of coffee while relaxing in the fragrant Bohemian air. A music pavilion was constructed across from the café and a children's playground was built, replete with fairy-tale friezes, sandboxes, wading pools, and a merry-go-round. An old movie theater was transformed into a concert hall and a building that had been used to treat children stricken in an encephalitis epidemic was repurposed as a social club, library, and synagogue. Shops were generously stocked with food from SS storehouses, kitchen utensils, used clothing, even suitcases. Most of the work, of course, was done by the prisoners themselves.

As the narrator in *Austerlitz* put it, Theresienstadt was turned into "a Potemkin Village or sham Eldorado which may have dazzled some of the inhabitants themselves." Meanwhile, the SS stepped up deportations to the death camps to alleviate overcrowding. In just a two-day period in May 1944, more than 7,500 "less presentable" prisoners were shipped to Auschwitz.[16]

I wonder what the prisoners made of this charade. Did they imagine that their tormentors had a sudden awakening and were now trying to make amends for their barbaric behavior? Did they allow themselves to feel even a glimmer of hope that they would somehow survive the nightmare of their captivity? Or, most likely, did they see it for what it was: a cruel and cynical hoax?

The Red Cross delegation arrived at the camp as scheduled on June 23, 1944. Following a precise timetable, they were escorted along walkways scrubbed clean that morning by the prisoners. They observed elderly residents sitting on benches reading books and children playing in the grass. They watched young men playing a soccer game as spectators cheered. They visited a dining hall where the food was served by white-gloved waiters. They listened to a jazz band named the Ghetto Swingers perform in the town square and attended a performance of a children's opera written by one of the residents.[17] Then, after six hours, they left.

The elaborate ruse was apparently convincing. The Red Cross inspectors issued a bland report that found little fault with the camp. It was so convincing, in fact, that the Nazis decided to make a movie about Theresienstadt for all the world to see. Directed by a prisoner named Kurt Gerron, an experienced actor and director who had appeared with Marlene Dietrich in *The Blue Angel*, the 90-minute film was titled *Theresienstadt: Ein Dokumentarfilm aus dem jüdischen Siedlungsgebiet* [Theresienstadt: A Documentary Film of the Jewish

Resettlement].[18] After filming was completed, Gerron and most of the cast and crew were dispatched to Auschwitz.[19]

In the fall of 1944, as the tide of the war turned decisively against Germany, the transports to Auschwitz and other extermination camps resumed in earnest. In a one-month period, between September 28 and October 28, some 24,000 inmates were deported.

Even after the ghetto was liberated by the Red Army, on May 8, 1945, the suffering and dying continued. As thousands of prisoners evacuated from other concentration camps poured into Theresienstadt, epidemics of typhus and other diseases swept through the town, killing scores of liberated prisoners along with doctors and other medical personnel and members of the Red Army.

All told, about 144,000 people, the vast majority of them Jews, passed through the gates of Theresienstadt between November 1941 and April 1945. Of that number, some 33,000 died in the ghetto, mostly from malnutrition and disease. Around 88,000 others were deported to Auschwitz or another Nazi extermination camp, where all but about 4,000 died.

PART IV

DAD'S SILENCE

When I was growing up I thought of the Holocaust as some horrible event that happened far in the past. Hitler and those wicked Nazis murdered my grandfather and millions of other Jews, but that was ancient history that had nothing to do with me or my immediate family. My father fled to the United States as a young man, met my mother, got married, raised a family, built a successful business, and made a good life for us. End of story.

That perception was reinforced by Dad's reluctance to talk about the past. He never spoke about his father or the other members of his family who were killed. Indeed, he hardly spoke about his life in Germany at all. It was as if his life had begun on that autumn day in 1937 when he walked down the gangway of the SS *Bremen* at the Hudson River piers.

The reality, of course, was different. I was born in 1951, just six years after the end of the war, eight years after my grandfather's murder, and 14 years after Dad had left Germany, so his memories of those harrowing events were still fairly fresh.

Researchers have found that Holocaust survivors tend to be divided into two camps: those who cannot stop talking about the horrors of the past and those who refuse to talk about them at all. My father clearly belonged to the latter. I always assumed his reticence was just a reflection of who he was, a quiet, unassuming man who didn't like to talk about himself or dwell on the past. It was only later, after he died, that I began to ponder the meaning of his silence and the impact that silence has had on me.

My late friend Karen Berman once wrote an article for the *New York Times* about the children of Holocaust survivors.[1] The article explained that the enormity of the trauma suffered by survivors often leaves an impenetrable void that is passed down from one generation to the next. Those in the next generation, Karen wrote, "often feel isolated and confused, caught up in a complex dynamic of grief, fear, anger, dislocation, and a sense of responsibility to somehow make up for their parents' losses."

Because so many of their relatives perished in Europe, children of Holocaust survivors often feel like they are growing up without a full family history. That feeling is heightened by a psychological phenomenon common among trauma victims called "snapshot memories," in which memories take the form of frozen images that have no beginning, middle, or end. As a result, children of Holocaust survivors hear bits and pieces of their parents' past but have trouble fitting them into a coherent narrative.

Some survivors are so distracted by memories of their own suffering and loss that they are unable to attend to their children's needs. Their children often grow up feeling insecure and unparented, and in some cases they find themselves parenting their own parents. Other survivors are so anxious and fearful about their children's well-being that the kids grow up feeling overprotected and emotionally smothered.

With my parents I experienced both of those poles. Dad tended to be aloof and emotionally detached while Mom was in your business 24/7. Their differences balanced out and helped cement their relationship, but they often left me feeling confused and conflicted. I yearned for more closeness with my father and dreaded being swallowed alive by my mother.

Karen's article noted that Holocaust survivors often experience violent nightmares and paralyzing flashbacks. Did my father ever have nightmares about being arrested at the French border and sent to prison? Did he ever wake up in the middle of the night while dreaming about a mob of Brownshirts storming the Kupfer villa? Did he have nightmares about his father being gassed or starving to death in a concentration camp? If he did, I never heard about it. I never saw Dad cry or express any strong emotions about the Holocaust. I never saw him cry, period.

What I do know is that my father kept his distance from Richard and me. Perhaps he was afraid to get too close to us because he wanted to spare us the pain of losing him, like the pain he must have felt when he lost his own father. Or maybe he was trying to protect himself from the pain of losing us when we got older and struck out on our own.

One of the few times the subject of Germany came up at home was during my senior year in high school. I had asked my parents if we could host an exchange student that summer and they agreed, but when I showed Dad the application, he noticed that I had checked Germany as one of several potential home countries. In my naivete I thought it would be great if we had a German student so Dad could speak to him in his native tongue. He quietly suggested I pick another country. We ended up hosting a young man from Sweden.

Passport photo dad

ON THE FENCE

I have struggled my whole life with bouts of depression and fear of intimacy. That's one reason I've been alone much of the time and my longest-term significant relationship was with a Labrador Retriever named Luke. Both of my parents loved me deeply, I have no doubt about that, but they also taught me to keep my distance from other people and be distrustful of the outside world.

A psychotherapist I saw for many years told me that when she first met me, I reminded her of a sarcophagus because I was so tightly wrapped and allowed so little outside light to penetrate my protective casing. Another therapist likened me to someone hiding in a dark room; I allowed people to glimpse me through the window, but if they got too close, I snapped the blinds shut. That's how I kept myself safe – and how I kept myself isolated and alone.

For many years I had a recurring dream of swimming along the coast and being swept out to sea by a powerful current as I frantically tried to get back to shore. I don't know much about analyzing dreams, but it doesn't take Freud to figure this one out. The shore symbolized safety and social conformity – that is, heterosexual love, marriage, and so on. The riptide represented my hunger for other men, a powerful, primal force that was beyond my control. I was desperately trying to follow the path I thought my family and friends expected of me, but my natural desires were pulling me away and I was terrified I would be lost forever.

I was deeply conflicted about my sexuality well into adulthood. It took me a long time to figure out who I was and what I really wanted. That confusion, I now understand, was largely sown by the shame I felt about being gay. Ambivalence was a way to avoid confronting reality.

In some ways my inability to express my own truth was a reenactment of how my father dealt with the trauma of the Holocaust. By not acknowledging my homosexuality, I was hoping that it would magically disappear; just as my father, by not talking about the Holocaust, was hoping that the trauma of those years would somehow fade away.

I never confided my struggles over my sexuality to Dad. Given that I was 25 when he died and had never been in a serious relationship with a girl, he probably had his suspicions. Naturally, I hoped he would accept me regardless of who I was attracted to, who I loved, but I was terrified that he would be deeply disappointed, if not devastated, if he learned the truth. I had nightmares that he and Mom would throw me out of the house.

I briefly had a girlfriend in junior high school, a sweet-natured Polish-American girl who was several inches taller and 20 pounds heavier than me, but for the most part I kept my distance from girls (and they from me). In college I occasionally dated girls and even had a few girlfriends – two of whom, to my parents' delight, were daughters of Jewish professors – but I was also aware of a growing attraction to men. Once or twice I wandered over to Madison's only gay bar and, from a safe distance, furtively observed the comings and goings of the clientele, most of whom were middle-aged men, but I never mustered the courage to go in.

In junior year I developed a secret crush on my roommate, a soft-spoken Jewish boy from Long Island whose father was a big *macher* in the Reform Judaism movement. Lenny[1] always seemed to have a girlfriend, and there were many nights when I would lay in bed, filled with lust and envy, listening to the amorous sounds emanating from his bedroom. I'm not sure if I was more envious of Lenny for having a girlfriend or of the girl for having Lenny.

It wasn't until after I left Madison that I wrote him a letter confiding my attraction to other men. Aside from a short letter and a brief phone conversation, I never heard from him again.[2] It was a pattern I saw repeated often: educated, enlightened people who were progressive on many social issues – civil rights, women's rights, even animal rights – but viewed gay rights as a bridge too far.

For a long time, into my early forties, I identified as bisexual. Unlike some closeted gay men I knew, my interest in women wasn't just a charade. I have felt genuine sexual attraction, at various times and in varying degrees of intensity, for the opposite sex, and when, as a young man, I succeeded in luring a girl to bed, I never had a problem performing and almost always enjoyed it. But as a practical matter, being bisexual left me in a perpetual state of limbo – neither fish nor fowl, gay nor straight. By sitting on the fence, I remained suspended between two opposing worlds, inhabiting neither.

GETTING CLOSER

During my freshman year at Wisconsin, Dad sent Richard and me a duplicate letter (I got the carbon copy) after a recent visit home. Richard and I were both in our High Hippie period, sporting long hair, flowery shirts, and frayed jeans, a look that didn't sit well with either of our parents. Richard wore his thick black locks in a ponytail and I bore a frightening resemblance to Tiny Tim, the scraggly-haired, falsetto-voiced ukulele player (who, as it happens, was the son of a Manhattan garment worker and the grandson of a rabbi).

"Let me briefly say that we greatly enjoyed your visit home and had it not been for the constant aggravation about HAIR it could be called perfectly delightful," Dad wrote, with typical diplomacy. He dispensed some business advice to Richard, who was making leather belts to supplement his college spending money, suggesting he "sell everything at reduced prices" rather than "losing the original investment." His advice might have reflected his own financial struggles. Business was slow, not a good thing when you're trying to put two kids through college.

He went on to express concern about his phone bill, which was $48 two months in a row, and suggested we keep future conversations short and to the point. "I would say by all means to continue to call, but before you do think out what you want to say and as you place the call ask the operator to notify you when three minutes are up," he suggested. "You be surprised how much you can say in three minutes if you make what you say count." A few days later, apparently after having second thoughts (or, more likely, Mom's intervention), he wrote another letter to Richard in which he walked back his earlier suggestion: "I realize that those telephone conversations are a therapy for both of us, however lengthy sometimes, and I take it all back." I don't recall if I received a similar reprieve.

Unbeknown to either Richard or me until months later, Dad was dealing with a far more serious issue than the phone bill. He had been diagnosed with lymphoma and was undergoing chemotherapy. The treatments left him red-faced, bloated, and fatigued, but they succeeded in driving the cancer into remission and enabled him to continue working and lead a relatively normal life.

A few years later, shortly after my 21st birthday, I wrote Dad a long, rambling letter reflecting my ambivalence about wanting to get closer to him while also yearning to strike out on my own. (It might also reflect the flowery prose I was reading in my 19th-century English literature class.) We were both on the cusp of big changes in our lives. I was due to graduate from college the following spring and Dad was contemplating taking his business in a new direction.

"I would like to get to know my own father better, and I look forward to it in the coming years," I wrote. "And yet ... spending too much time at home would put definite limitations on my personal growth." I expressed no such ambivalence, however, about my admiration for him and my gratitude for the lessons he had taught me over the years:

"You have instilled in me the most basic and important truths in life – love, dignity, personal strength, integrity, patience, and so much more. I am not sure what I am looking for in life, but whatever it is, these same values are fundamental to whatever I discover or create. Your life, your being, has been, and will always be, a constant inspiration to me. Just knowing what you are gives me greater strength, more vitality, than all the knowledge I have acquired in this world, than any of the distinguished intellectuals, artists, and common people I have encountered. I see your life as a celebration of the human spirit. And there is nothing higher, nothing holier than this. ... I love you very much."

After my senior year at Wisconsin I moved back to my parents' house in Hamden and got a job driving cab in New Haven.[1] It was hardly my dream gig, but the economy was in recession and good jobs were hard to come by. Besides, after four years of toiling in academia I enjoyed the mindless monotony of driving a taxi and the opportunity to meet ordinary people living ordinary lives.

Dad didn't say anything when I announced my new job at dinner, but I could tell by the tight set of his face and his downcast eyes that he was disappointed. Mom was less circumspect.

"Is this why we sacrificed all those years to send you to college, so you can drive the *schvartzas* around town in a *farshtunken* taxi?" she asked. "Why don't you get a respectable job, a job with a future?"

"Mom, it's only for the summer, until I figure out what I'm going to do."

"What you're going to *do*? Isn't that why we sent you to college in the first place, so you could figure out what you're going to do?"

The following summer I decamped to Manhattan to pursue my twin passions of writing and photography and, more urgently, to get away from Big Gert. I pictured myself roaming the gritty streets of Gotham with my trusty Rollieflex, capturing "decisive moments" a la Henri Cartier-Bresson, my favorite photographer. At night, in my spartan downtown loft, I would develop prints in the ruby gloom of a makeshift darkroom and hunt-and-peck a literary masterpiece. In my free time I would mingle with writers, painters, and other artists at recherché boîtes and Soho soirees.

My mother, unsurprisingly, didn't share my bohemian vision. "New York is no place for a young man without a job," she warned.

"Do you have any idea how much it costs to live in that city? And the crime! The *schmutz*!"

She looked over at Dad, who was calmly reading the *Times*. "Bob, talk some sense into your son."

"If the boy wants to live in New York, who are we to stop him?" he replied, peering over the top of his newspaper. "He's old enough to make up his own mind."

The morning of my departure Mom made a last-ditch effort to talk me out of going. It was mid-June and the Northeast was already in the grip of a stifling heat wave. Glancing at the thermometer outside the kitchen window, she let out a low hiss. "Look at that temperature! It's almost 80 degrees already!" she announced as if reading a breaking news bulletin. "It's *meshugge* to move to New York in this heat! Can't you at least wait a few days until it cools off?"

But my mind was made up. I knew that, as far as my mother was concerned, there would never be a good time for me to move to New York, or anywhere else for that matter.

Outside Union Station, Dad gave me a firm handshake and a reassuring pat on the back. Mom, on the other hand, acted as if I were going off to war in a faraway land rather than a city 75 miles down the line. She wrapped her long arms around me and pulled me into her trembling bosom. Tears rolled down her cheeks and dripped inside the collar of my shirt. "Take care of yourself, darling," she sniveled in my ear. "And call us as soon as you get there."

I moved into the Penington, a Quaker rooming house in a dog-eared brownstone on East 15th Street, around the corner from the red-brick Friends Meetinghouse on Rutherford Place. With its cast of oddballs and misfits, the Penington was an ideal place to be introduced to the wonders and weirdness of New York City. The *dramatis personae* included a children's book author from the Midwest who spoke with a British accent for no apparent reason; a middle-aged psychotherapist from Geneva who was having an affair with a handsome young black dancer from the Alvin Ailey dance company; a dancer with Les Ballets Trockadero de Monte Carlo, the all-male comic ballet troupe; an aspiring Irish playwright prone to tearful rants and violent rages; and a one-time Catholic seminarian whose new calling seemed to be the attempted seduction of every resident equipped with a penis.

During those early years in New York I essentially led a double life – a nice, straight Jewish boy by day, a lusty homo by night cruising for sex in the dark crevices of the city. A typical evening out might begin with dinner or drinks with friends and end up in the back room of a gay bar or at Man's Country, a gay bathhouse on West 15th Street that offered a variety of venues – from a tractor-trailer truck to a prison cell and a military barracks – for sexual encounters.

After cavorting into the wee hours, I would stumble home through the deserted streets, past the crackheads and winos slumped on park benches in Union Square, consumed by feelings of guilt and shame. I pictured my parents sleeping in their comfortable suburban home and wondered what they would think of their youngest son roaming the predawn streets of Manhattan like a wild animal returning from the hunt. I imagined they would be dismayed and disgusted. I thought about dying.

After a year or so of living among the Quakers, queers, and other Peningtonians, I decided it was time to get my own apartment. It was a big decision for a 24-year-old earning a meager salary as a proofreader. Dad sent me a letter detailing the potential costs of such a move. I suspect it was written at the insistence of my mother, who was alarmed at the prospect of my living alone in the Big City.

"*To help you decide whether or not to maintain a new apartment I have made inquiries and here are the factual results on a monthly basis,*" he wrote. He then listed the following projected expenses:

- *Cost of rooms: $200*
- *Food $16*
- *Telephone $40 (6 months waiting time)*
- *Kitchen utensils $8*
- *ConEd Electricity (light cooking) $12*
- *Linen service $12*

- *5 Shirts [laundered] weekly @50¢ $10*
- *Insurance Camera-Darkroom $20*

Total monthly cost $318

I'm not sure where he got the idea that I would require "linen service" because I always did my own laundry. And as for budgeting $16 a month for food, even in 1975 that seemed like an unrealistic amount. I ended up renting a fourth-floor walkup on West 85th Street near Riverside Drive for $225 a month. I ate a lot of sausage and eggs.

FINAL DAYS

In the spring of 1976, Dad's lymphoma came back with a vengeance. He began to suffer from fatigue and intermittent fevers and was in and out of the hospital for days and sometimes weeks at a time. Richard moved back home to help Mom take care of him and I took the train up to New Haven almost every weekend.

Adding to Dad's woes, his long-time business partner, Herb Setlow, had decided to phase out Crown Shirts as a separate entity and incorporate its product line into a division of the parent company. Under the reorganization, Dad was to work only one day a week as a consultant. Whether the move was prompted by his declining health or some other reason, I don't know, but he wasn't thrilled with the arrangement.

Among Dad's papers I found a letter he had drafted to Herb while he was in the hospital seeking to renegotiate the terms of his new contract. "I would find it hard and do not intend to live on $300 a week," he wrote. "If you would pay me $300 for one day's service you would be wasting your money. I don't enjoy lazy money. I enjoy earning it."

Removing him from the day-to-day operations of the business, Dad argued, would be a big mistake. "Soon the business would feel the absence of direction, orders would dry up, the whole operation would grind to a halt with only the empty shell of a meaningless contract remaining."

He urged Herb to give him a larger role in the reorganized business. "I sense we are at the threshold of new and important developments and I feel quite capable of producing very substantial income. So I feel this is the wrong time to cut back on my services."

I don't know whether this letter, or some form of it, ever made it into Herb's hands, but it certainly doesn't sound like the words of a man who was expecting to die anytime soon.

One Sunday morning when I was visiting with Dad in his bedroom he motioned for me to come closer. He was lying in bed, his head propped up by several pillows.

"Let's go to the shore," he whispered in my ear.

The request took me by surprise. He hadn't been out of the house in weeks except to go to the doctor or the hospital, and he was so weak he could barely lift his head. The mere act of uttering those few words left him short of breath.

Mom naturally tried to talk him out of it. "Oh, darling, that's too far," she cooed like a disapproving schoolmarm.

"No," he rasped, defiantly. "I want to go."

Richard and I helped him out of bed. Sick as he was, he insisted on dressing for the occasion. We shimmied a pair of trousers over his spindly legs and pulled a shirt and cardigan over his sunken chest. Even though it was a warm summer day, we caped a coat around his shoulders for good measure. Richard guided him down the steps to the garage and gently lowered him into the front seat of the car while I arranged a few throw pillows around his head and shoulders and laid a wool blanket over his lap.

Richard, normally a speed demon, drove with uncharacteristic restraint. Mom and I sat silently in the back seat while Dad, his head barely visible above the headrest, looked straight ahead. Occasionally he would turn his head to take note of children playing in front of their house or someone walking their dog, but he kept his thoughts to himself, or perhaps he was too weak to speak.

We took the back roads to the Sound, snaking through East Rock Park, past the sloping meadow where we once coaxed kites into the sky in fall and raced sleds in winter. We drove past our old house on Willow Street, rattled over the Ferry Street drawbridge into East Haven, and followed the narrow, winding roads hugging the coast, past salt marshes, weathered stone manors, and shambly summer cottages. We passed the entrance to the Colony Beach Club, where we once whiled away endless summer days swimming, playing tennis and ping-pong, and wolfing down grilled hot dogs chased with fizzy rasp-lime sodas that tickled our noses. In Guilford we circled the town green, past Colonial-era brick and clapboard houses and a classic white-columned church, and followed Old Whitfield Road down to the water.

"Let's go," Dad said in a surprisingly spry voice as Richard parked across from the dock.

"Darling, it's so windy today," Mom said, clutching the collar of her jacket. "Don't you think you'd be more comfortable staying in the car?"

But Dad shook his head and clicked open his seatbelt. Richard helped him out of the car and guided him toward the seawall. In the harsh glare of the afternoon sun, the toll the disease had taken was brutally evident. The erect posture he always prided himself on had given way to a slumped shuffle. His raincoat hung loosely around his shrunken frame, flapping in the stiff breeze thrumming off the Sound.

A man sitting on a bench saw us coming and got up to give Dad his seat. Mom and I sat down on either side of him while Richard wandered off, lost in his own thoughts. We sat there for a long time, gazing silently at the gray water and the tumbling gulls. The air felt as thick as maple syrup and everyone seemed to be moving in slow motion.

I thought about the many times we had come to Guilford to

celebrate special occasions – Mother's Day, Father's Day, birthdays. We would go to the Stone House, just down the road, to feast on clam chowder and steamers, baked stuffed lobster and soft-shelled crab, and strawberry pie *mit Schlag* (as Dad used to say). After dinner we would walk along the pier, past the weathered gray lobster pots stacked along the seawall and the sailboats bobbing in the harbor.

I looked over at Mom and saw tears glistening in her eyes. A bitter lump welled in my throat. It was our last family outing.

Dad tried to keep his illness secret as long as possible. No one outside close family was told except his business partner, and I don't think even Herb was aware of the seriousness of his condition until near the end.

I was visiting him in the hospital one day when a woman I had never seen before knocked on the door of his room. Before I could explain that he wasn't seeing visitors she breezed past me and called out a cheerful greeting. Moments earlier Dad had been lying in bed, too weak to utter more than a few words, but to my amazement he responded in a clear, firm voice. She carried on an animated monologue for several minutes as he stared at her, occasionally nodding his head.

When the woman finally left, I asked, "Who *was* that?"

He glanced at me, looking utterly spent. "I was about to ask you the same thing."

Whenever I visited Dad in the hospital he always greeted me with a smile, even though I could tell he was in pain. Despite all the discomfort he was in, the countless tests and procedures, the ceaseless pricking and prodding, the pills and more pills, he rarely complained. "I'm fine," he would say whenever I asked him how he was feeling. Occasionally he would get annoyed with a careless nurse or an indifferent aide, but his gentle demeanor and impish sense of humor somehow survived the indignities of his disease.

But in the last few weeks I noticed a change. He became more irritable and sometimes openly hostile toward my mother and the hospital staff. It was a side of him I had never seen before. One of the nurses suggested the powerful meds he was taking were probably to blame.

One afternoon when I was visiting him he wiggled his fingers, beckoning me closer. "Tell them to stop with the painkillers," he whispered in my ear.

"How come, Dad?" I asked, trying not to show my surprise.

"I don't want to go home a drug addict," he replied.

And that was the attitude he held until the end, that he was going to get better and go home. If he ever came to terms with the terminal nature of his disease, he gave no sign of it. The closest I heard him come was to say, "I don't think I can fight it anymore." Another time, as he held my mother's hand, he plaintively asked, "Momma, what's going to be with us?" But the next day he was talking about going home again.

Shortly before he died the doctors performed a biopsy to determine if the cancer had spread to his lungs. After the procedure I spent the night with him in the ICU. As I stood by his bed holding his hand, surrounded by the blinking lights and the clicking, humming sounds of machines, I felt both intense love and numbing fear. I wasn't religious and had serious doubts about the existence of God, but that didn't stop me from praying silently – to whom, I don't know – that he would get better.

Dad's eyes were closed, but I could tell by the way he pressed my hand that he knew I was there. He was obviously in terrible pain. Every breath he took was accompanied by a low, quavering moan. I later learned that some of his doctors didn't expect him to make it through the night.

A few days later Mom told me she saw Dad cry for the first time since he got sick. "He thought they had taken out his lungs," she said.

The following week I sent him a note in the hospital. Either I was a good liar or I, too, was incapable of accepting reality:

"Just wanted to let you know I'm thinking about you and pray that your recovery continues on a steady course. I know you're still suffering a great deal of pain and discomfort, but all the doctors seem agreed that the worst is now over. I know they're right. So try to put on a happy(er) face and think about the whole family being together again, <u>at home</u>. Dad, there has never been a day in my life when I haven't felt proud to be your son. Look forward to seeing you this weekend. Much love, Peter"

The last time I saw my father was on a Sunday evening in mid-September. I had visited him in the hospital that morning but, not feeling well myself, hadn't stayed long. After dinner I decided to drive down to the hospital again before taking the train back to New York early the next morning. I seldom visited him at night, but perhaps I sensed it might be my last chance to say goodbye.

I arrived around 9:30 and found him alone in his room. The private nurse we had hired to look after him at night had stepped out. He was curled up on his side, his head resting on the corner of the pillow. His eyes were closed so I sat down in the aqua-colored vinyl chair next to the bed and watched him in silence. In the dim glow of the hospital light, his face looked as pink and smooth as a baby's.

After a few minutes I leaned forward and whispered, "Hi Dad." He opened his eyes and looked at me with a puzzled expression. I'm not sure if he was disoriented or just surprised to see me at such a late hour. "What are you doing here?" he rasped. "Go home."

He dozed off again. After a few minutes he opened his eyes. "Are you going home now?" he asked in a soft, barely audible voice.

"Yeah, I better go," I replied, as I leaned over and kissed him on the forehead. "I'll see you soon, Dad. I love you."

I was playing bridge with friends at the Penington a few days later when I got a call from Richard on the pay phone in the basement –

the only phone available to residents. Dad had passed away that afternoon. He was 69 – the same age his father had died in Theresienstadt, and the same age I am as I write this.

I told Mom I would take the late train to New Haven, but she told me to wait until the next day. "There's no point in coming tonight, darling," she said in a low, gravelly voice. "It's late. There's nothing you can do. Come tomorrow."

I walked back upstairs in a daze. My friend Nancy wrapped her arms around me and suggested we take a walk. We wandered aimlessly around the neighborhood, west on 15th Street, then north on Irving Place past historic Pete's Tavern, with its red bricks and black awning,[1] and around Gramercy Park. A tranquil private enclave shaded by ginkgo and oak trees and bordered by stately brownstones and townhouses, Gramercy was one of my favorite refuges in the city, a place I often repaired to when I was feeling sad or depressed.[2]

I was grateful that Nancy was with me. She was one of my best friends in New York and one of the few who had known my father. She had come with me to Hamden on several occasions to visit my parents. She was charmed by Dad's courtly manner and meticulous dress, and he was equally taken with her warm personality and striking appearance – a reed-thin former model, she stood six feet tall and sported a stylish orange pixie.

We ended up at a coffee shop on Third Avenue, which, like almost every coffee shop in New York in those days, was run by Greeks. As I nursed a Coke and Nancy sipped tea, I talked about how proud I was of Dad and how much I would miss him. I reminisced about all the good times we had spent together in New York, going to Broadway shows and Lincoln Center concerts, visiting the Guggenheim and Metropolitan museums, eating at the Carnegie Deli and Lüchow's, the renowned German restaurant by Union Square.[3] I recalled the afternoon my parents picked me up outside the General Motors building on Fifth Avenue, where I was working as a proofreader at a law firm, proudly pimped out in an iridescent blue suit I had recently acquired in an East Village boutique. Mom gasped when she saw my outfit; Dad just chuckled.

Nancy encouraged me to let out my feelings, but, like my father, that wasn't something I was very good at. I felt overwhelmed by sadness, but I couldn't bring myself to cry. And I was frightened of what laid ahead. By the time we got back to the Penington it was late and everyone had turned in. We tip-toed up the creaky staircase, hugged goodnight, and slipped into our respective rooms.

Dad and me, circa 1968

Dad in New York, 1968

THE GOOD CHINA

The morning after Dad's funeral the house was eerily quiet, the air heavy and still. Mom and I walked around in a trancelike state, avoiding eye contact and taking pains to make as little noise as possible. If we didn't speak, if we moved very slowly, perhaps we could avoid the reality that he wasn't coming home again.

Aunt Nan and her daughter Jean were coming over for lunch, and Mom asked me to set the table in the dining room, normally reserved for special occasions. I took down Nana's good china, the bone-colored plates with the scalloped blue border, from the top shelf of the kitchen cabinet and collected the stainless steel silverware from the drawer.

As I was setting the table, I felt a burning sensation in the pit of my stomach. Why were we having guests for lunch? Why were we eating at all? The person I loved most in the world was lying in a cold dark box and we were acting as if it were just another day. It made no sense to me.

Mom emerged from her bedroom wearing a plain dark dress. Her hair smelled of chemicals from the hairspray that held her dyed brunette bouffant in place.

"Can you zip me up, honey?" she asked wearily, turning her back to me.

As I pulled up the metal clasp, I thought of all the times I had seen Dad perform the same task. He had always taken pride in the way Mom put herself together when they went out. She was a smart dresser who tended to wear simple dresses and classic suits set off with a silk scarf and a few pieces of carefully chosen jewelry – a single strand of pearls, gold earrings, an animal brooch with jewel-encrusted eyes.

She glanced over her shoulder at the table. "Oh, darling," she sighed. "Why didn't you use the *good* silver? We're having company. You know better than that."

Dutifully, I walked over to the walnut buffet and pulled open the top drawer. The sterling silverware, dull and dusty from disuse, lay forlornly in velvet-lined compartments. As I began to gather the pieces, something snapped.

"Why do we have to use the good silver?" I shouted, flinging the silverware back into the drawer with a clatter. "What the hell difference does it make? It doesn't fucking matter."

Mom looked at me, her face taut with disappointment. "Oh, Peter, not now. They'll be here any minute."

But the fuse had been lit. I slammed the drawer shut and bolted out the front door, nearly knocking over Nan and Jean, who were coming up the front walk carrying trays of food. I kept my head down but out of the corner of my eye I could see the surprised expression on their faces.

"Peter!" Mom called out from behind the screen door. "Where are you going?"

But I didn't answer. I stalked around the neighborhood in a blind rage. Part of me felt guilty for upsetting my mother, but another part felt relieved, even glad, that I had given voice to my true feelings.

I ended up at Bassett Park, a few blocks from the house, where we used to watch Richard play Little League. I tramped into the woods and curled up against the trunk of an old oak tree. After all the time spent indoors at the hospital, the house, the funeral parlor, the synagogue, it felt good to be outside in the fresh air.

For the first time since Dad died I allowed myself to cry. I cried for the father I would never see again. I cried for the mother I could not imagine ever smiling again. And I cried for myself, for the emptiness and uncertainty that lay ahead.

I don't know how long I stayed in the woods, but it must have been several hours because by the time I got home Nan and Jean were gone. The dishes and good silver were washed and put away.

PART V

GUEST OF THE CITY

In 1989, a decade after my first visit to Weiden, I returned to Dad's hometown for the third time. This time I came as a guest of the city, which had invited former Jewish residents to celebrate the centennial of the synagogue and commemorate the local victims of the Holocaust. Aunt Teddy, the widow of my father's brother Ernst, who lived in Paris, was also invited.

Nineteen former residents and their families attended the five-day event, which received extensive coverage in the local press. It was a moving experience to meet these former friends and neighbors of my father's family who were now scattered around the globe, from England, France, and Israel to the US, Canada, and the Dominican Republic. I was proud to represent the Kupfer clan, but as always when I visited Dad's hometown, my feelings were tinged with sadness and longing.

The opening reception was held at Stadtverwaltung Weiden, the city's modern new City Hall. It featured an exhibition about the Jewish community, including brief histories and photographs of each of the families attending the event. The section on the Kupfers noted the importance of the family glass business and displayed photos of Otto and the Kupfer villa. The headline in *Der Neue Tag* the next day read: "*Verstehen ist Basis fur die Zukunft.*" [Understanding is the Basis for the Future.].

The next morning we visited the Jewish cemetery, which had been spruced up for the occasion, the grass and shrubs neatly trimmed and the graves adorned with fresh-cut flowers. Some visitors had tears in their eyes as they viewed, perhaps for the first time, the graves of their relatives, but there wasn't as much emotion displayed as one might expect, perhaps because they felt uncomfortable showing their feelings in the presence of reporters and other observers. Afterward, Teddy and I had lunch at the home of Jewish community leader Hermann Brenner and his wife Henny, where we were joined by their son Michael and Max Adler, an elderly gentleman who was the son of a former business associate of my grandfather.

That evening we attended a lavish banquet at the Altes Rathaus, in a grand hall with carved stone archways and ornate chandeliers hanging from the timbered ceiling. *Oberbürgermeister* Hans Schröpf introduced Hermann Brenner and other Jewish leaders as well as members of a local Christian-Jewish association that had sponsored the event. Then the mayor delivered a long-winded speech welcoming the guests and discussing the history of the Jewish community in Weiden. As he mentioned each guest, he asked them to stand as everyone applauded. Given that I had never lived in Weiden and was a generation younger than the other guests, I felt self-conscious when my name was called. It was my father, not me, who should be here, I thought, my father, not me, who should be getting this recognition. But stand I did.

The mayor went on to describe the changes that had occurred in Weiden since the war and expressed the hope that everyone, Jews and Gentiles alike, would come to terms with the past and put it behind them. Then we enjoyed an epic feast of smoked salmon, roast beef, lamb chops, cheeses, breads and cakes, washed down with an assortment of German wines.

After dinner two former residents addressed the gathering. Walter Krell, whose family had owned the largest department store in Weiden, lived in London, and Hermann Steiner lived in San Diego.

They spoke in German, so I understood little of what they said, but the impact of their words was plain to see – people laughed, cried, grinned, and grimaced. Steiner, who appeared to be in his seventies, later told me that he had known both my father and grandfather, but he seemed reluctant to talk about them, or perhaps his memory failed him after so many years.

My old friend Inge covered the event for *Der Neue Tag*, where she was now the chief editor. After dinner I walked over to her office as she was putting the finishing touches on her article. Then we went back to the composing room to watch the printers lay out the story on large boards, a process I later became familiar with as a composing room editor at the *San Francisco Chronicle*. The article included a picture of Teddy and me standing in front of the Kupfer grave. On another page, under the headline *"Peter Coopers grosse Hoffnung!"* [Peter Cooper's Last Hope!], was a story about my efforts to recover the portraits of Eduard and Fanni, which appeared next to a reprint of Inge's original article about Frau Fischer and the paintings from 1979.

Shortly before arriving in Weiden for the reunion, I received a letter from Inge with some surprising news. Both Frau S. and her husband had died since my last visit and the portraits had been inherited by their son, a man I'll call Hubert. Inge had approached Hubert, who worked at a local bank, about turning the paintings over to me, but, like his mother, he was demanding a sizeable sum of money. He had also approached DETAG, the last company to own the Weiden glass factory, about buying the portraits, but they failed to reach an agreement.

But Inge was as determined as ever to get the paintings back. "Peter, we can't give up now!" she declared. "These pictures must be returned to your family!"

She was trying to raise money through private donations to buy the paintings. In the meantime, she had spoken to the mayor again and he had promised to try to persuade Hubert to surrender the portraits.

After putting the paper to bed, we drove to the Hotel Stadtkrug to see our friend Dieter. Despite the huge meal I had eaten a few hours earlier, he insisted on serving us an assortment of cold cuts, cheeses, and other snacks, washed down with copious amounts of beer, wine, and brandy, topped off with champagne. It was a wonderful evening and I was more than a little drunk by the time Dieter had one of the waitresses drive me back to my hotel around 3 a.m.. As I have observed many times over the years, Bavarians love their food and drink, and while I share their passion, I'm a lightweight when it comes to alcohol. Whenever I'm in Weiden, I seem to be *shicker* more often than not.

The next day we were taken by bus to the synagogue in Floss, which had only recently reopened after being nearly destroyed on Kristallnacht. The mayor gave a speech and then the chief cantor of Berlin's Jewish community sang a few hymns. A short, heavyset man with a large head and bulging eyes, he looked a bit like Shrek, but there was nothing cartoonish about his voice. With his hands slicing the air around him, he sang in a rich baritone that pulsed with emotion.

Then we went to Flossenbürg, where a survivor of the camp gave an emotional speech recounting his experiences. He lamented that the site, now adorned with flowers, fountains, and sculptures, fails to convey to young Germans the unvarnished truth about the atrocities that were committed there. During lunch at a community center in Floss we were presented with a book about the thousand-year history of the city and a porcelain plate commemorating the restoration of the synagogue.

In the evening we attended a concert in Weiden where the cantor from Berlin sang again. As he lifted his head toward the sky and spread his arms, you could almost feel the sea parting. The music, needing no translation, touched me in ways that words could not. Like Dad, I am not given to displays of emotion, but the cantor's powerful voice and gestures brought tears to my eyes. I cried for my family and I cried for all the people whose lives were destroyed by Hitler and his evil Reich.

The next morning Eduard Wittmann dropped by my hotel. Dressed in baggy pastel-colored pants and a worn suede coat, he looked more like a hardscrabble farmer than the prosperous businessman he was. He greeted me with his endearing, gap-toothed smile, warm and effervescent as ever, and presented me with a beautifully illustrated book about the Bavarian glass industry, which included reproductions of the portraits of Eduard and Fanni and a drawing of the Kupfer manor in Frankenreuth.

On the last morning of the event we gathered at a small park near the city center for the unveiling of a tall granite slab commemorating the local victims of the Holocaust.[1] After the ceremony Inge introduced me to an elderly woman who held a framed photograph of a middle-aged man. "We have never forgotten your grandfather," she said, tears glistening in her eyes, as she tugged on my shirtsleeve. "He gave my father-in-law a job when he was out of work and struggling to feed his wife and four children." I was deeply touched that, after more than half a century, she still remembered my grandfather and had taken the trouble to attend the ceremony.

Despite all the kindness the people of Weiden had shown me and the other guests, the ceremonies and speeches, the concerts and receptions, the bountiful food and drink – or perhaps because of it all – I was feeling lonely and depressed by the end of the week. As was the case in my previous visits to Weiden, I was caught up in a swirl of activity that left me little time to relax or reflect. My emotions were all over the place, careening from joy and gratitude one moment to sadness and guilt the next.

The root of it, I suppose, was that I didn't feel I deserved any of the attention I was getting. The only reason I was being wined, dined, and feted was because my grandfather and other members of my family – people I had never even met – had been murdered. It didn't help matters that I didn't speak German, so I couldn't understand much of what was being said at the official functions or in casual conversations and had to rely on people translating for me.

Communicating with Aunt Teddy was also a challenge because she spoke almost no English, and my French wasn't much better.

I also sensed that some of the other guests resented Teddy and me because we had no direct ties to Weiden. While other guests had brought their spouses and children along, they had to pay their own way. Teddy and I and the other official guests had most of our expenses covered by the city, including airfare, accommodations, and most of our meals.

To make matters worse, Teddy was driving me nuts. A Polish Jewish refugee who had met Uncle Ernst in France before the war, she was a strong-willed, resourceful woman who had made a small fortune as a wine dealer. She lived in a spacious, modern apartment overlooking Parc des Buttes Chaumont in northeast Paris and owned a handful of other apartments around the city. I had stayed with Teddy several times when visiting Paris and she had always been very kind to me, so I was looking forward to seeing her again. But it didn't take long for her to start boasting about how much money she made and how many apartments she owned. Then she started grilling me about how much money I made, how much rent I paid for my apartment in New York, and when I was going to get married – to a nice Jewish girl, of course!

On our last day in Weiden, I ran into Teddy outside the Rathaus. She had just come from seeing the mayor and showed me a bill of sale for three cases of wine she had sold him (presumably on behalf of the city). I loved my aunt and admired her entrepreneurial drive, but I felt she was taking advantage of the mayor's hospitality and it embarrassed me. This was neither the time nor place to be doing *gesheft*.

But there was something else bothering me. I felt that so little had changed in my own life since my first visit to Weiden a decade earlier. I was 37 and still alone, still struggling to establish my career as a journalist, and still confused about my sexual identity. In short, I felt like a failure whose only claim to fame was the murder of my grandfather and other members of my family.

EDUARD AND FANNI RETURN

In the spring of 2006, my cousin Erich invited me to join him on a trip to Germany. Erich, who was 13 years younger than my father, had grown up in Munich and fled to the United States in November 1938, a year after Dad (and only a few days before Kristallnacht!). His father Karl, one of Otto's younger brothers, and his mother Selma were both murdered in Auschwitz.

I always enjoyed spending time with Erich, not just because he was my father's closest relative in the US but because his appearance and mannerisms reminded me so much of Dad. Medium height with a full head of white hair, a formidable nose, and a healthy paunch, he had the same guttural accent, mischievous sense of humor, and fondness for hearty meals capped by calorie-laden desserts. And, like Dad, he had also been in the *schmata* business, only he made ladies' dresses instead of blouses.

I had fond memories of meeting Erich and his wife Ruth in Munich during a previous trip to Europe many years earlier.[1] While Ruth went shopping, her favorite pastime, on fashionable Maximilianstrasse, he took me on a long walking tour of the city. He showed me the apartment building on Schwanthalerstrasse where he and his parents had lived (he was an only child) and where his father, a doctor, had his medical office. Then we walked to the soccer stadium where he had watched matches as a boy, the grounds of Munich's famed Octoberfest, and the Jewish cemetery where members of his family were buried. Although I was in my early thirties and Erich was more than 30 years my senior, I struggled to keep up with him and was ready to *plotz* by the end of the afternoon. We capped the day at a traditional Bavarian restaurant near Marienplatz where Erich remembered eating with his parents and my father and grandfather. As we dined on Wienerschnitzel and Weissbier, surrounded by a boisterous crowd on the terrace, I felt a shudder of sadness as I pictured Dad and his father sitting in the same place – perhaps the same table – half a century earlier.

While we were in Munich I decided to call Inge at *Der Neue Tag* to say hello. It had been years since we last spoke. The receptionist at the newspaper told me Inge had retired, but she promised to let her know that I was trying to reach her. Sure enough, a few hours later I got a call from Inge at our hotel.

It didn't take long for our conversation to turn to the subject of Eduard and Fanni's portraits. After so many years, I had all but given up hope of ever recovering them, but Inge got fired up all over again. "Peter, we must find out what happened to those paintings!" she exclaimed. She promised to make some inquiries and get back to me.

Several weeks later, after I returned to San Francisco, I received an email from Inge with news that Frau S.'s son Hubert still had the portraits. A week later came a second email confirming the first: "Both paintings are in Weiden! They are hanging in the dining room of Frau S.'s son. Every day he and his family are admiring the portraits of Mr. and Mrs. Kupfer."

My cousin Paul, another great grandson of Eduard and Fanni, wrote a letter to Hubert asking him to return the paintings. Two weeks later Paul received a startling response from his wife, a woman I'll call Audrey: her husband had been killed in a motor scooter accident near his home a few days earlier. "With a very heavy heart," she wrote, she would return the paintings to the Kupfer family so that they "will again find a place where they belong."

Paul and I were thrilled at the prospect of getting the paintings back, but now we had to decide what to do with them. Eduard and Fanni had 10 children who survived into adulthood, and their descendants were scattered across Europe, the United States, and South America (and probably other places we don't even know about). Who among us should get the pictures? We considered donating them to the municipal museum in Weiden or to a Jewish museum elsewhere in Europe or the US. But after much discussion we decided that, after being separated from the family for so many years, they should be returned to the fold.

Although I was eager for our family to reclaim the pictures, I wasn't particularly interested in hosting them myself. I live in a small apartment in San Francisco with little room for a pair of large oil paintings. Besides, formal 19th century portraits didn't fit my aesthetic. So it was decided that Paul would take them back to his home southeast of London for the time being, and eventually they might travel to the homes of other family members.

In June of the following year, I met Paul and another cousin, David Mangel, a grandson of Ernst and Teddy from Paris, in Weiden. The day after we arrived the three of us drove to Frankenreuth to visit the site of the original Kupfer glassworks. Not much had changed since my first visit in 1979 except a few new houses and other buildings had sprouted up. The sprawling white manor where my grandfather and his many siblings had grown up was still there. So was the small rose-colored church with the large wooden crucifix hanging over the door. The old *glashütte* was completely gone. All that remained was an overgrown field that was being used by a local gun club.

That afternoon we met Inge and her husband, Waltfried Wirtz, whom she had married since my last visit to Weiden. Coincidentally, Waltfried had recently retired as the managing director of a local mirror-glass manufacturer and he had arranged for us to tour the float glass factory in the neighboring town of Weiherhammer – the factory that had rendered the Weiden foundry obsolete. It was a huge complex with a pair of towering smokestacks that could be seen from miles around. As we approached the entrance Paul, David, and I were tickled to see the British, French, and American flags flying from poles outside the main gate.

We were greeted by the factory director who gave us a brief overview of the operation in flawless English. He was obviously very proud of his high-tech plant, which ran around the clock, producing huge sheets of plate glass that were shipped all over the world. Then he walked us around the complex, which was several football fields long. We took an elevator to the top of one of the 7,000-foot cooling towers, which offered a spectacular view of the countryside almost as far as Prague, more than 100 miles to the east.

That evening we had dinner at Waltfried and Inge's home in a leafy village outside of Weiden. They lived in a modern, multilevel house built into a hillside with an indoor pool and a lush garden in the rear that sloped down to a large pond. We ate in a dining room with a high peaked roof and expansive windows that gave the impression of being in a fancy treehouse. Inge had prepared a delicious dinner of beef goulash, spätzle and – special for me, she said – Knödel, the airy potato dumplings my father and I both adored, capped by a creamy torte swimming in raspberry sauce and a bottle of Mosel wine.

The next morning Inge picked us up at our hotel. As we drove to Audrey's house on the outskirts of the city, chills darted up and down my spine. It was hard to believe that nearly 70 years after my grandfather had been forced to give them up and more than a century after they had been painted, the portraits of Eduard and Fanni were about to be reunited with their family.

Audrey was waiting for us on the doorstep of her modest, well-kept rowhouse. A short, stout woman with close-cropped gray hair, she greeted us with a wave and a shy smile and led us into the house. It didn't take long to spot the portraits. Set in matching antique-gold frames, they were hanging regally above the sofa, commanding the attention of anyone who entered the room. Eduard and Fanni's heads were angled toward each other, as if to meet each other's gaze. Eduard, sporting a neatly trimmed gray beard, a dark velvet jacket with wide lapels, a high-collared white shirt, and wide gold tie, looked every bit the captain of industry that he was. Fanni, wearing a ruffled black dress trimmed with white embroidery, looked equally imposing. Her dark hair was pulled back in a tight bun and her eyebrows were slightly arched, as if she were about to pose a question.

It was a strange feeling to finally see the portraits in the flesh, so to speak, after knowing them for so many years only through the 5x7 reproductions Inge had sent me. Considering all they had been through, they were in surprisingly good shape. Audrey explained that her husband had the paintings restored and placed in new frames. With the exception of a few cracks and blemishes on Fanni's face, one would never have guessed that they had spent decades hidden away in what was likely less than optimal conditions.

As a black-eyed calico cat named Felix looked on, Audrey explained that her 15-year-old daughter had been riding on the back of the motor scooter her husband was driving when the fatal collision occurred. The girl wasn't seriously injured but had total amnesia about the accident and had been struggling in school ever since. It was impossible not to feel sorry for this unassuming woman who was clearly still in shock from the recent loss of her husband and was struggling to cope with her daughter's trauma.

Audrey was obviously not happy about giving up the paintings, which had been in her husband's family for so many years and were the centerpiece of her living room, but she was never less than gracious. She insisted that she hadn't known who the subjects of the paintings were until she received the letter from Paul. All she knew, she said, was that her husband had inherited the portraits from his parents who, in turn, had inherited them from Frau S.'s aunt, Emma Fischer, my grandfather's housekeeper.

When we took the pictures down from the wall, however, we found some papers tucked behind one of them that told a different story. They were faxed photocopies of extracts from Dr. Schott's dissertation about the Jewish community in Weiden, with passages about the Kupfers highlighted in yellow.[2] The faxes had been sent by the Weiden municipal archives in January 2006 – less than two years earlier – so clearly Hubert had been aware of the provenance of the paintings, even if his wife had not.

We presented Audrey with framed copies of the reproductions Inge had made along with a letter signed by Paul, David, and me extending our condolences for the loss of her husband and thanking her and her family for caring for the paintings and agreeing to return them to us. David also gave her a bottle of French wine.

When we got back to the car the three Kupfer cousins exchanged high-fives. "*Wunderbar!*" Inge exclaimed. "At last the paintings are back where they belong." Then we drove to Inge's golf club for a celebratory lunch – a celebration decades in the making – and drank a champagne toast to Eduard and Fanni.

That evening, as I stood alone on the balcony of my hotel room in Weiden, I thought about the long journey that had brought me there. It took more than a quarter-century from the time I first heard about the existence of Eduard and Fanni's portraits to finally get them back. Amid all the losses the Kupfers had suffered as a result of the Holocaust, salvaging this piece of the family legacy felt like a small but important victory.

And, of course, I thought about my father. I'm sure he would have been proud of what my cousins and I had done. I pictured him looking down on us and smiling, and I felt closer to him than I had in a long time.

The return of Eduard and Fanni would not have been possible, of course, without Inge's help over the years. I've often wondered what it was about those paintings that inspired such persistence. When I posed that question to her recently, she sent me a long email in response:

"*When I saw the two pictures of Peter Kupfer's grandparents for the first time, I was fascinated not only by the perfect painting technique, but primarily by the charisma emanating from the couple portrayed, who modelled for the artist with dignity and elegance, but also with friendly nobility. The two portraits were miraculously saved throughout the turmoil of World War II and the turbulent post-war period. Why couldn't this likeable couple spend their old age in peace? How did the atrocities to which the people of my country allowed themselves to be carried away become possible?"*

Inge was apparently confusing my grandfather Otto, who died in the Holocaust, with his parents Eduard and Fanni, both of whom died many years before Hitler came to power. But that didn't diminish the power and poignancy of her words. To her, the portraits were symbolic of the millions of Jews murdered by the Nazis.

After the war, Inge wrote, she became preoccupied with the question of how "the barely endurable atrocities – above all against the Jewish people" were allowed to occur. "I was 10 years old at the time, so I was a child, but newspapers or publications of all kinds attracted my attention more than dolls and other toys. I kept asking my mother why no one took the Jews under protection. Why they and their contemporaries watched these deadly activities and did not intervene."

Inge described her mother as "an incredibly kind woman with a lot of heart who helped every refugee or needy person who knocked on her door." But she always insisted that she was unaware of what was happening to her Jewish neighbors. "I didn't know!" her mother would tell her. "We were told that the concentration camps were filled with murderers and other serious criminals." Her father, who was employed by Deutsche Reichsbank, the national bank, and had somehow "succeeded in not having to join the party (NSDAP)," was under the same impression.[3]

"So my parents were certainly not involved in the events of the Nazi era," Inge continued, "but I – as their child – was still ashamed. Perhaps that was one of the reasons why I really wanted to see the two beautiful pictures restored to their traditional place with the Kupfer family. Why I 'fought' for it by every means."

TEREZÍN TOURIST

On May 2015, 72 years after my grandfather's death in Theresienstadt, I boarded an intercity bus in Prague for the 40-mile trip northwest to Terezín. The bus was crowded with a mix of tourists and locals. Young men wearing yarmulkes stood in the aisle kibitzing in Hebrew while middle-aged couples studied guidebooks and others read newspapers or gazed out the window. Outside the city, the landscape quickly turned pastoral, the checkerboard of flat green and brown fields punctuated with vast swaths of yellow rapeseed and stands of oak.

The bus dropped me off opposite the old town square, a large plaza framed by a double row of linden trees and crisscrossed by dirt paths that converged on a lifeless fountain in the center. An austere Empire-style church stood on the northeast side of the square, its bell tower rising solemnly above the town.

In garrison days the square had been used to stage military parades. After the Nazis took over Terezín in 1941 and transformed it into a Jewish ghetto and work camp, the plaza was enclosed in barbed wire and a large circus tent was pitched to house a *Kistenproduktion,* or box-making factory, where hundreds of prisoners toiled in cramped, squalid conditions. The handsome neoclassical buildings flanking the square were occupied by SS headquarters, prisoner barracks, and various other ghetto functions.

It was a gorgeous spring day, warm and sunny, but the square was oddly deserted. As I looked around, trying to get my bearings, the other passengers who had gotten off the bus with me seemed to vanish. I walked across the square toward a canary yellow building with a large sign reading "Memorial." I figured this might be the ghetto museum, but it turned out to be a hotel and, like almost everything else in Terezín, it seemed to be abandoned.

According to its website, the Memorial is a "luxurious four-star hotel" with a "beautiful neo-renaissance ballroom" and a "presidential apartment." It seemed odd to find such a fancy hotel in such a bleak place, but tourists – even those visiting a former concentration camp, I suppose – like their creature comforts. The website included a brief history of the building, but it conveniently omitted the fact that it had been occupied by the Nazis during the war. Exactly what function it served is not clear, but the building next door, now a bank, had been SS headquarters where prisoners were interrogated and tortured in basement bunkers.

I found the museum around the corner in a two-story building enclosed by an iron fence. The entrance, up a short flight of stairs, was marked by a Hebrew inscription I couldn't read. Inside the lobby a dour gray-haired woman collected the admission fee – 225 Czech crowns, or about $10 – without so much as a word or nod of acknowledgement. I felt a flash of anger as I plunked down the money. Surely the Czech government could have figured out another way to finance the museum other than charging admission, especially given that many of the visitors were probably people, like me, who had come to pay respects to their murdered relatives. Adding insult to injury, a separate fee was required to visit the Small Fortress and other parts of the ghetto, and a crude map cost an additional 10 crowns.

Czechs are not known to be a cheerful lot – they rarely smile or make eye contact with strangers – but the museum staff made the people I encountered in Prague seem positively effervescent. When I asked a guard for directions to the screening room, she sneered as she pointed the way, seemingly annoyed that I would bother her with such a silly question. Indeed, the staff, mostly matronly women, looked as if they themselves were prisoners, and in a way I suppose they were. After all, ghetto tourism, for lack of a better term, seemed to be the town's main industry. The few businesses I came across – the hotel, a few restaurants and bars, an ice cream shop – catered to visitors, and most of them were closed that day.

Judging from the sullen attitude of most of the people I met, they resented living and working in a town whose main claim to fame is that it had once been a Jewish ghetto. And who can blame them? Who would want to live in a place where thousands of men, women, and children had been held captive, tortured, and killed, and where a steady stream of visitors was constantly reminding you of that ignominious history?

Still, I didn't feel much sympathy for them. Unlike my grandfather and the other Jews who were forced to live and die in Theresienstadt, no one was compelling these people to live there now, so the least they could do is be civil to visitors.

The museum building, which originally served as a school, was used by the Nazis to house ghetto children. The first floor paid tribute to these young victims, displaying a list of the thousands of children who died in the camp as well as the drawings and poems they made during their captivity. The drawings seemed surprisingly normal, even rosy – pictures of mountains, trees, and flowers, children and dogs playing under a smiling sun. But few of the young artists would live to experience such simple pleasures again. Of the 15,000 children who passed through the gates of Theresienstadt, only about 1,100 survived.

While I was visiting the museum, it was invaded by a busload of boisterous middle-school-age students. They were gaily chatting, laughing, and horsing around as if they were on a field trip to the zoo. I felt my body stiffen and the blood drain from my face. Didn't these kids have any sense of decency? Didn't they realize that they were cavorting in front of the pictures of children who had been robbed of their childhood and wantonly killed? I kept waiting for their chaperones or the museum staff to rein them in, but no one said a word.

The last straw came in a room containing a scale model of the camp. Several kids were punching buttons that illuminated different functions of the camp – the railroad siding where the deportees arrived, the mortuary, the crematorium – as if they were playing a video game, while their classmates looked on, laughing. "Excuse me!" I practically shouted as I elbowed my way through the pack and glared at the boys playing with the buttons. They got the message and moved on, but one boy looked back at me as he was leaving and loudly muttered, "Stupid English!"

The experience made me wonder how much had really changed since the Holocaust. Young people were disrespecting the memory of thousands of murdered Jews while the authorities blithely looked the other way. Had these kids not learned anything? Had they not been taught anything? The atmosphere was different in Berlin, where I had been before going to Prague. My visit coincided with the 70th anniversary of the end of World War II, and there were many exhibitions and other events throughout the German capital commemorating the war and reminding the public of the atrocities committed by the Nazis. The visitors I observed seemed genuinely interested in learning about that monstrous chapter in their history. And in Paris, where I went the following week, a group of schoolchildren touring the Museum of the Shoah behaved with appropriate solemnity.

The second floor of the museum was devoted to the ghetto as a whole and the Holocaust in general. It showed the familiar grisly pictures of hollow-eyed prisoners and piles of skeletal remains. The

Nazi devotion to detail was evident in documents noting the reason for each prisoner's arrest, when and how they were transported to the ghetto, and what happened to them after they arrived.

I studied the exhibits, looking for any sign of my grandfather, in word or image, but found none. Of course, it would have been difficult to recognize the well-groomed, impeccably dressed man pictured in my father's photo album among the photographs of cadaverous prisoners on display in the museum.

After touring the exhibits I sat alone in a small hall off the lobby and watched a film about the ghetto. It contained excerpts from the so-called documentary the Nazis made about Theresienstadt, showing carefree residents dancing, gardening, and attending concerts and plays.

Then, map in hand, I set out to explore the town. It was eerily quiet except for the intermittent sound of hammering in the distance. The streets were deserted save for a young boy aimlessly pedaling his bicycle. In a park across from the museum a disheveled old man stumbled around, muttering to himself. A young woman wheeled a baby carriage past a crumbling stone wall with a sign pointing to the crematorium. A man walked hand in hand with a small boy past the entrance to the mortuary.

As I walked around, I tried to imagine what my grandfather's life had been like in the ghetto. As an elderly man he might have been spared the most physically taxing work like digging graves or hauling rocks. Was he consigned to cobbling shoes or sorting rags? Did he work in the box factory or the delousing station? Or perhaps he was already too frail and sick to do anything but lie in the infirmary and wait for death to take him.

Around the corner from the ghetto museum, facing the north side of the square, stood the old Town Hall, an ornate French Imperial-style building that had served as the ghetto courthouse. On the west side of the square another neo-Renaissance building, which had housed the *Ghettowache, or* ghetto guard, was now a cultural center.

Down the street stood a sprawling salmon-colored building the Nazis had used as a barracks for old people and an auxiliary hospital.

Was this where my grandfather had spent his final days? When I walked into the lobby I was confronted by a scowling woman behind a glass partition. "Hospital! Hospital!" she snarled. Clearly, I was not the first tourist to wander into the building uninvited. I asked if this was where old people had been housed in the ghetto, but she just shook her head and muttered, "Nothing, nothing."

On the south side of the square, next to the Hotel Memorial, a building that had once served as the ghetto café was now occupied by a secondhand store. The shop was closed, but through a thick film of dirt covering the window I could make out piles of miscellaneous items – kitchen appliances, dishes and utensils, coats and other clothes. In *Austerlitz*, the narrator suggests that some of the items in this shop might have belonged to the prisoners. Did one of my grandfather's silk ties or monogramed shirts, I wondered, lay among the farrago of used goods.

On the northeast side of the square, next to the church, stood another classical-style building that had served as a barracks for young girls and a rehearsal space for the ghetto orchestra. On the opposite side of the church stood a lemon-colored colonnaded building that had functioned variously as SS headquarters, a post office, and a barracks.

After walking around the square, I headed south to the railroad siding, where prisoners arrived from the west or were sent on to death camps to the east. The rail spur connecting the ghetto to Bohusovice was built in 1943 – by the prisoners themselves, of course – to speed up the deportation process. I sat down on a grassy slope near the tracks, wrapped my arms around my knees, and bowed my head. I tried to imagine what my grandfather and the other prisoners must have felt when they emerged from the dark, fetid railroad cars and found themselves in this desolate field. For the first time since arriving in Terezín, I cried.

After a few minutes I got up and walked to the mortuary. It was there that the prisoners prepared the dead for burial, ritually washing their bodies and placing them in rough-hewn wood coffins. But as the corpses piled up, even this concession to Jewish custom was abandoned. The prisoners were conscripted to build a crematorium so the bodies could be disposed of more efficiently.

I followed a narrow, tree-lined path that opened onto a wide field studded with graves. A large stone menorah stood toward the rear of the cemetery. The only sound was the rustling of leaves in the breeze and the occasional chirping of a bird.

To the left stood a long, low yellow stucco building with a row of small windows below the roof line. The crematorium began operating on September 7, 1942, more than three months before my grandfather died, so his body was almost certainly among the tens of thousands consumed there.

Inside it was cool and quiet except for the sound of my footsteps echoing off the thick masonry walls. Four hulking black metal furnaces, two on each side of a narrow aisle, gave off a dull sheen. Next to them stood metal ramps that had apparently been used to feed the corpses into the flames. I lit a white prayer candle and placed it next to several other candles burning on one of the ramps. As I said a silent prayer, the magnitude of the evil that took place in Theresienstadt hit me full force. Tears welled up, but I wouldn't allow myself to cry in front of those silent black monsters.

By the time I returned to the town square it was after 5 p.m. I decided not to go to the Small Fortress, which was a 20-minute walk across the river. After spending the afternoon visiting one chamber of horror after another, seeing countless photographs of brutalized prisoners and stony-faced SS guards, I had had enough. I was hungry, tired, and emotionally spent.

I missed the bus back to Prague by a few minutes and the next one, the last of the day, wasn't scheduled to arrive for an hour and a half. I walked around town looking for something to eat, but the only place I could find open, other than the ice cream shop, was a pub. I sat at an outside table next to three men who were drinking beer, smoking, and bantering loudly in Czech. As I wolfed down a Wienerschnitzel with boiled potatoes and a beer, I couldn't help thinking that the simple meal I was enjoying would have been considered a feast by my grandfather and the other prisoners.

On the bus back to Prague I wondered, not for the first time that day, how so much evil could have been perpetrated in such a serene place. Did no one – an SS officer, a guard, a clerk – see a starving boy and slip him a crust of bread? Did no one see a hysterical mother clutching her child and try to comfort her? Did no one see a frail old man and offer him a potato.

BACK TO WEIDEN

The next day I took a bus to Nuremberg, getting off in front of the city's monumental neo-Baroque railroad station, and boarded a train for Weiden. As we snaked through the countryside, past villages with tidy stucco houses and hills studded with stands of silver-gray beech trees, I was struck once again by the lush beauty of Bavaria. And once again I felt a creeping melancholia knowing that my father had been forced to flee this beautiful land, leaving so much behind.

I thought back to my first visit to Weiden and the excitement I had felt as I uncovered bits and pieces about Dad's early life – and the excitement I had felt about my own life and the possibilities that lay ahead. But as I watched the bucolic landscape slip by my window, I felt as if much of that early promise had gone unfulfilled. Yes, I had carved out a decent career as a journalist. I had traveled the world, photographing and writing stories about the people and places I encountered. And I had made some good friends and forged a few intimate relationships along the way. But at that moment I was alone, with no partner, no family, and no job, and my life didn't feel very settled or satisfying. I had hoped to bring my own children to Bavaria one day to show them where their grandfather was born and grew up, but that wasn't meant to be either.

When I got off the train in Weiden, Inge was waiting to greet me, just as she had many times in the past. It had been almost eight years since our last meeting, when Paul, David, and I had come to reclaim the portraits of Eduard and Fanni. She had turned 80 in December, and though she still had that familiar twinkle in her eyes she was beginning to show her age. Her husband Waltfried had died several years earlier and she herself had had a series of medical issues. She walked with a halting gait, but that didn't stop her from playing golf nearly every day. In fact, she was quick to inform me, she was playing in a golf tournament the next day, so she wouldn't have much time to spend with me this visit.

We dropped off my bags at a hotel overlooking Marktplatz, then drove to the site of the old *Glasfabrik*. Although the factory had been closed for years, remnants of the brick complex were still visible, partially hidden behind some newer buildings. I tried to get closer to take some pictures, but a security guard shooed me away, warning that photographs were not permitted.

As we walked back to the car, Inge, ever the resourceful journalist, remembered that she knew a woman who lived in one of the houses next to the foundry. A few minutes later I was standing barefoot on the woman's bed, snapping pictures of the factory through an open window. "Typical man," Inge quipped when I inadvertently stepped on one of the pillows.

Then we drove down the street to the site of the Kupfer villa to take some more pictures. It was now occupied by a modern office building, three or four stories high. Next door, the Wies transportation agency was gone too, replaced by another office building.

That evening we had dinner at Inge's golf club, on a terrace overlooking the course. As we dined on Wienerschnitzel and Kartoffeln (Bavarian-style roasted potatoes with bits of sausage), Inge talked about the war and the Holocaust. Even then, after so many years had passed, she found it hard to believe that all those "terrible, terrible things" had happened. She wasn't denying that they had occurred, of course, but she was still incredulous that such atrocities could have taken place in her homeland, and not so many years ago. In the days and weeks after the war ended, she recalled, the city was flooded with desperate refugees seeking food and shelter. "I was just a little girl," she said, a bewildered look flashing across her face. "I didn't understand what was happening."[1]

After dinner she took me on a tour of the club grounds in a golf cart. The higher elevations offered panoramic views of the countryside around Weiden, with the smokestacks of the Weiherhammer glass factory visible in the distance. Then we went back to town to have dessert at an outdoor cafe on Marktplatz, not far from the street where she grew up. As the bells from a nearby church tolled, she smiled wistfully. "I remember hearing those same bells when I was a child."

The next day Dr. Schott, the city historian who has been so helpful to me in researching my father's family, met me at my hotel. Over coffee in the dining room he talked about the final days of the war and the fate of the Kupfer villa. Although the house had been occupied by Nazi officials at the time it was struck by American artillery, he didn't think it had been deliberately targeted. He suspected the attack was intended to show the Germans that the Allies were closing in rather than an effort to inflict any serious damage on the city. Only a handful of buildings, in addition to a tower in the old city wall, were hit, and, unfortunately, the villa was among them. The next day, April 22, 1945, the German army fled the city, leaving the local militia to formally surrender to the American troops.

Then we walked to the synagogue a few blocks away. It was Saturday and the Sabbath service was just ending. There were only about a dozen people in attendance, mostly older men in their fifties and sixties. We were introduced to the cantor, an energetic young man in his early thirties who was originally from Siberia. He told us there were about 300 Jews then living in Weiden, most of them Russians who had settled there after the war. Sebastian and I shared a toast with the worshippers before they sat down for their Sabbath meal.

On Sunday, my last day in Weiden, Werner Friedmann, the son of the elderly shopkeeper I had met during my first visit in 1979, met me at my hotel. His father had long since died and now he ran the men's clothing shop on Marktpatz. Werner told me antisemitism was still an issue in Germany. A few years earlier a youth gang had swooped into Weiden and stirred up trouble, defiling property with antisemitic graffiti, but since then there had been no major problems. "The city has been very supportive of the Jewish community," he said. "They provide police protection outside the synagogue and the Jewish school. Whenever we need something they are there to help us."

Then we drove to the Jewish cemetery on the outskirts of town, which had grown noticeably more crowded since my last visit. After the war, when there were so few Jewish families left in the city, a portion of the cemetery land had been sold off. But now, with the influx of Eastern European Jews, the community was running out of space and recently purchased additional land next to a Christian cemetery outside the city to accommodate the overflow.

The large pinkish-gray Kupfer headstone stood toward the rear of the cemetery, with the family name inscribed in gold. But something had changed since my last visit. Eduard's name and dates had been added, as had those of my grandparents Otto and Berta. Why was Otto – who died in Theresienstadt and whose remains were almost certainly not in Weiden – added to the inscription, while his mother Fanni – who died in Weiden – was not? I haven't the faintest idea. Nor did I ever find out who commissioned the new engraving, though I assume it was paid for by members of the Jewish community.

I stood silently in front of the grave for several minutes. Although I had never met any of these people, after all my visits to Weiden, after hearing their stories and studying so many old pictures and documents, I felt as if I knew them all. And, though he was buried thousands of miles away in New Haven, I felt my father's presence too. I gathered several stones and placed them on the headstone.

When we got back to the hotel Inge was waiting for us in the dining room. After breakfast she took out her notebook to interview me for one last article in *Der Neue Tag*. Apparently, she wasn't as retired as I thought she was.

Then a social worker from the Jewish community, a Russian woman named Marina Jurowetzkaja, dropped by to discuss the possibility of placing *Stolpersteine* [stumbling stones], at the site of the

Kupfer villa in memory of Otto and Mina. The brainchild of German artist Gunter Demnig, tens of thousands of the small concrete cubes have been placed around Germany and several neighboring countries. Each contains a brass plate inscribed with the name and life dates of a victim of Nazi persecution. Marina explained that some members of the Jewish community were opposed to *Stolpersteine* because they believed it was disrespectful to allow people to walk on the commemorative stones, but she promised to discuss it with the president of the community and let me know.

Then I gathered my bags and Inge took a few more pictures outside the hotel before driving me to the *Bahnhof*. As we walked into the station she insisted on buying me a warm buttered pretzel, her favorite snack as a child, from a street vendor.

As we stood on the platform waiting for the train she presented me with a beautiful leather wallet that had belonged to Waltfried. She remembered that I had lost my own wallet on the U-Bahn in Berlin shortly before arriving in Weiden. I nearly cried with gratitude. As we hugged goodbye, I half expected her to say, "See you later, alligator," but she just smiled and said, "*Auf Wiedersehn.*"

As the train pulled out of the station the red-brick remnants of the old glass factory glided past my window. I grabbed my camera to take a picture but wasn't quick enough. Then I settled in for the long ride to Paris via Nuremberg.

On my second day in Paris I woke up to a jarring email from Inge. She had had a heart attack the day after I left Weiden and was in the hospital. When I called her she told me that she had arrhythmia and may need to have surgery to implant a pacemaker. Naturally she sounded a bit upset, but she seemed to be in good spirits.

After we hung up I arranged to have flowers sent to her room – not an easy task when you're in one foreign country ordering flowers in another. I couldn't help wondering if the excitement of my visit might have contributed to the attack. After her golf tournament on Saturday we had had a late dinner together, and then she had met me at the hotel the next morning.

The following week Inge's article about my latest visit to Weiden appeared in *Der Neue Tag* under the headline "*Der Enkel Hat*

Vergeben" [The Grandson Has Forgiven]. Something was apparently lost in translation because I don't recall using those words. What I did say was that I was grateful for having made some good friends in Weiden – Inge foremost among them – and that I considered the city "like a second home."

Article in Der Neue Tag, 1979

ARTICLE 116

On a sunny November morning in 2019 my niece Ariel and I stood outside an imposing black iron gate in front of the German Consulate in the tony Pacific Heights neighborhood of San Francisco. We rang the bell and a guard quickly appeared and beckoned us in. We walked through a courtyard landscaped with a small pond and abstract sculpture and entered a handsome orange-brick Georgian Revival townhouse.

We had come to the Consulate for an unlikely purpose – to be interviewed as part of the process of applying for German citizenship. Under Article 116 of the German constitution, adopted in 1949, the descendants of former German citizens who were deprived of their citizenship on political, racial, or religious grounds during the Nazi era are eligible to have their citizenship "restored."

I had long been aware of the law but had never seriously considered applying for German citizenship until Ariel, my brother's younger daughter, started the process. As I helped her gather the necessary documents, I decided I might as well join the party. Although I had no intention of ever living in Germany, I have often thought about living elsewhere in Europe, and having citizenship in an EU member state would surely make that a lot easier. Moreover, given the political climate in the US, with Trump in the White House and his white supremacist minions running amok across the land, the option of living in another country had become increasingly appealing.

The receptionist directed us to a large room with floor-to-ceiling windows offering a panoramic view of the Bay. After a few minutes a young man casually dressed in a sports shirt and slacks walked in and introduced himself. Jonas was soft-spoken and polite, a pleasant departure from the brusque, officious manner I associated with German bureaucrats.

I had brought a folder of my father's old documents – birth certificate, passport, immigration papers, and so on – in anticipation of being grilled about our eligibility for citizenship. But after spending a few minutes reviewing our applications and asking a few innocuous questions, Jonas said everything seemed to be in order and there was nothing further we needed to do. Although it normally took about a year to process the applications, he cautioned that due to an unusually large backlog it might take considerably longer.[1] Then he stood up, shook our hands, and wished us luck. And that was it.

Outside, Ariel and I took a selfie smiling next to a brass plaque reading "Consulate General of the Federal Republic of Germany" and posted it on Facebook. A few minutes later the Consulate posted a comment under the photo: "Congratulations!"

As we walked back to the car, I couldn't help wondering what Dad would make of what we were doing. His son and granddaughter were applying to become citizens of a country from which he had narrowly escaped with his life. A country responsible for the murder of his father, numerous aunts, uncles, and other relatives, and millions of other Jews. Could he have imagined that his homeland, once ruled by an antisemitic psychopath, would one day emerge as one of the world's staunchest democracies, while the US, once a paragon of democracy that had provided safe haven to him and millions of other refugees, would fall under the sway of a fascistic xenophobe?

AFTERWORD

Like many children of Holocaust survivors, I grew up with a gaping hole in my family history. With the exception of my cousin Erich in New York and a few other cousins in France and England, I never knew anyone from my father's side of the family. Even my mother's family was shrouded in mystery because her parents left behind much of their own history when they fled Ukraine at the turn of the last century.

Through the process of writing this book I have gained a clearer picture of who my father was and the forces that shaped him. And I have gained a stronger sense of who I am and how I fit into the world. Knowing Dad's story has made me feel more rooted and less elusive. It has also helped to bridge the divide that kept us apart. Strange as it may sound, in some ways I feel closer to him now than I did when he was alive. It's been a long journey, but I feel richer for having taken it.

The Holocaust might have been an abstract event to me and other children of survivors, but to my father it was all too real. It influenced everything he did, everything he thought, how he presented himself to the world. His reserved manner, meticulous appearance, wariness of outsiders, even his detachment from his own sons, was no doubt influenced by the trauma of his early years.

Although we were very different people, with different strengths and weaknesses, different lifestyles and sexual identities, I would like to think we shared some of the same traits – honesty and integrity, belief in social justice, capacity for hard work, and last but not least, a puckish sense of humor.

Since moving to San Francisco in 1992, I have been living as an openly, and proudly, gay man. I have a small circle of multicolored, multitalented friends, gay and straight. Coincidentally or not, several of my closest friends are German-born Gentiles and my partner of the past six years is the product of a German father and a Venezuelan mother, neither of them Jewish. And I am still in touch with my friend Inge, who is now midway through her ninth decade, and a few other people in Weiden.

I'm not sure what Dad would make of all my German connections. I imagine he would be less than thrilled, but I also think he would be proud of me for following my own path and trying to live up to the values he instilled in me.

In the spring of 2022, around the time I found a publisher for this book, I learned that the Jewish community in Weiden had finally reached an agreement with city officials to have *Stolpersteine* placed at the site of the Kupfer villa. In addition to Otto and Mina, memorial stones will also be laid for seven other siblings who perished in the Holocaust – Johanna, Berta, Moritz, Karl Michael, Friedrika, Robert, and Rosa.

And because the mission of the Stolpersteine project is to "reunite" families torn apart by Nazi persecution – including those who survived the Shoah but were forced to flee their homes – my father and his brother Ernst will also be commemorated.

As of this writing, the installation, with Gunter Demnig himself in attendance, is scheduled to take place in November. Ariel and I, along with several other descendants of Eduard and Fanni Kupfer, plan to be there.

ACKNOWLEDGMENTS

This book would not have been possible without the help and support of many people and organizations.

First of all, I want to thank my cousin Paul Sinclair, who was indispensable in helping me track down, translate, and interpret documents about my father's family ferreted from public and private archives and his own personal collection. Paul translated several of the letters between my father and grandfather that I found in my parents' attic, a discovery that inspired this book.

I am indebted to Dr. Sebastian Schott, the historian in Weiden's Office for Culture, City History, and Tourism, for his generous help in researching my father's family and the Jewish community in Weiden. Sebastian was incredibly patient in answering my endless (and no doubt annoying) questions and confirming (or not) the information I gathered.

This book really began on the September morning in 1979 when I stumbled onto the offices of *Der Neue Tag*, the newspaper in Dad's hometown, and was introduced to a fellow journalist named Inge Roegner. Inge took an immediate interest in my story and has written numerous articles over the years about my quest to uncover the world my father left behind. She was also instrumental in helping me reclaim the portraits of my great grandparents Eduard and Fanni Kupfer. That chance encounter marked the beginning of a friendship that has lasted more than four decades, and hopefully will continue for years to come.

I am grateful to the late Eduard ("Eddie") Wittmann for introducing me to the natural beauty and rich culture of the

Oberpfalz and for that unforgettable day in Pleystein, Frankenreuth, and Regensburg.

My thanks to Dr. Michael Müller for allowing me to draw on his extensive research of the Bavarian glass industry and, in particular, of the Kupfer family's involvement in the industry. Thanks also to Dr. Michael Brenner – who even when I first met him as a teenager in Weiden more than 40 years ago showed signs of becoming the distinguished professor of Jewish history he is today – for giving me a sense of what life was life for Jews in Weiden during the Nazi era. Bernhard M. Baron, the former head of Weiden's Office for Culture, City History, and Tourism, was also helpful in painting a picture of when Weiden "went brown."

Jackie Pels, my former copydesk mate at the *San Francisco Chronicle,* provided early encouragement, wise counsel, and last but not least, a brilliant title. The irrepressible founder and sole employee of Hardscratch Press, Jackie specializes in stories about Alaska, but she can tell a good yarn about anywhere, anything, and anyone.

My late colleague at the *Bridgeport Post* in Connecticut, Karen Berman, a gifted writer, loyal friend, and single mom extraordinaire, was an insightful early reader and enthusiastic supporter of *Glassmaker.* I only regret that she is not here to see the final product.

My German-American *Freund* Franziska Marks carved out time from her busy life to translate some of the correspondence between my father and grandfather, among other documents. Marion Hedger, my favorite psychic, refused to allow me to abandon this project, even when I despaired of ever finding a publisher. Thanks for your steadfast support, Blubs. Thanks also to Nancy Fern, Debbie Diamond, Wolf Breiman, and members of the Barbary Coast Book Club for reading early drafts of *Glassmaker* and providing valuable feedback.

I am grateful to my cousins Jean Adnopoz and Susan Ray for clarifying bits and pieces of my family history, and to Marcie Setlow and Carrie Setlow for their warm reflections about Dad (the feeling was mutual).

Thanks to Jude Richter and Megan Lewis of the US Holocaust

Memorial Museum; Rachel Shapiro, Valery Merlin, and Karin Dengler of Yad Vashem; Wolfgang Spahr of the Düsseldorf City Archives; Dr. Till Strobel of the Amberg State Archives; Albina Mayer-Hungershausen of the Hessen State Archives; Heike Drummer of the Jewish Museum Frankfurt; Angelika Rieber of Projekt Jüdisches Leben in Frankfurt; Sigrid Kämpfer of the Institute for the History of Frankfurt; Pamela Elbe of the National Museum of American Jewish Military History; the late Marvin Bargar of the Jewish Historical Society of Greater New Haven; and Ed Surato of the New Haven Museum.

I am also grateful to the Opus House Writers' Retreat in Truchas, New Mexico, and the Wellstone Center in Soquel, California, for providing two very different but equally inspiring spaces to reflect and write.

My late therapist Charlotte Melleno paved the road for this book with a few simple words: "Peter, you need to tell your story." Thanks also to Justin Hecht and the members of the Sacramento Street men's group and to Alan Kubler for their support.

Marcia Rockwood provided incisive editing and, more importantly, helped me understand what this book is really about: a search for identity – my father's as well as my own. And thanks to Liesbeth Heenk and Amsterdam Publishers for believing in *Glassmaker* and bringing it to life.

Last but not least, thanks to Waldemar and dearly departed Luke (a/k/a Boobies) for putting up with me all those years my eyes were glued to my computer screen and my fingers were tapping deep into the night.

SELECTED BIBLIOGRAPHY

Bayer, Karl and Bernhard M. Baron. "*Weiden 1933: Eine Stadt Wird Braun*" [Weiden 1933: A City Goes Brown]. *Oberpfälzer Nachrichten*, 1983. Republished Spintler Druck und Verlag, 1993.

Berenbaum, Michael. *The World Must Know: The History of the Holocaust as Told in the US Holocaust Memorial Museum*. 2006.

Bondy, Ruth. *Elder of the Jews: Jakob Edelstein of Theresienstadt*. Grove Press, 1989.

Brenner, Michael. *Am Beispiel Weiden: Jüdischer Alltag im Nationalsozialismus*. Wurzburg: Arena, 1983.

Kurinsky, Samuel. *Glassmakers: An Odyssey of the Jews: The First Three Thousand Years*. Hippocrene Books, 1991.

Harris, James F. *The People Speak! Anti-Semitism and Emancipation in Nineteenth Century Bavaria*. University of Michigan Press, 1994.

Heger, Heinz, *The Men with the Pink Triangle: The True Life-and-Death Story of Homosexuals in the Nazi Death Camps*. Alyson Books, 1994.

Henderson, Bruce. *Sons and Soldiers: The Untold Story of the Jews Who Escaped the Nazis and Returned with the U.S. Army to Fight Hitler*. William Morrow, 2017.

Hohenhaus, Peter. "Flossenbürg Concentration Camp Memorial Site." Dark Tourism. Accessed June 13, 2022. https://www.dark-tourism.com/index.php/15-countries/individual-chapters/218-flossenbuerg-concentration-camp.

Kater, Michael H. "Everyday Antisemitism in Pre-War Nazi German." Yad Vashem. Jerusalem, 1984. Accessed June 13, 2022. https://www.yadvashem.org/odot_pdf/microsoft%20word%20-%205618.pdf.

Klemperer, Victor. *I Will Bear Witness: A Diary of the Nazi Years, 1933-1941*. New York: Random House, 1998.

Laschinger , Johannes. "Judenpogrome in Weiden und Amberg 1938". Historical Club for Upper Palatinate and Regensburg, 2016.

Levy, Esther. *Legacies, Lies and Lullabies: The World of a Second Generation Holocaust Survivor*. Design Publishing, 2013.

Luhrssen, David. "The S.S. Bremen: Last Voyage of a Luxury Liner." Warfare History Network. Accessed June 13, 2022. https://warfarehistorynetwork.com/2016/11/11/the-s-s-bremen-last-voyage-of-a-luxury-liner/.

Marrus, Michael R. *The Unwanted: European Refugees in the Twentieth Century*. Oxford: Oxford University Press, 1985.

Müller, Michael. "Die Spieglas Dynastie 'Kupfer und Glaser' und die Glastütte Frankenreuth" [The Kupfer and Glaser Glass Dynasty and the Frankenreuth Glass Foundry]. Translated by P. Sinclair. Rijo Research, 2012. http://www.rijo.homepage.t-online.de/pdf_2/EN_BY_JU_frankenreuth.pdf.

The National Archives [UK]. "The Holocaust: Theresienstadt." Accessed June 16, 2021. https://www.nationalarchives.gov.uk/education/resources/holocaust/theresienstadt/.

Oertel, Arthur Karl Heinz. "Holocaust Encyclopedia." United States Holocaust Memorial Museum. Accessed June 13, 2022. https://encyclopedia.ushmm.org/content/en/id-card/arthur-karl-heinz-oertelt.

Reuben, David. *Everything You Always Wanted to Know About Sex* (*But Were Afraid to Ask)*, McKay, 1969.

Schott, Sebastian. *Weiden a Mechtige Kehille: Eine Jüdische Gemeinde in der Oberpfalz vom Mittelalter bis zur Mitte des 20 Jahrhunderts*, Translated extracts by P. Sinclair. Pressath: Eckhard Bodner, 2003.

Sebald, W. G. *Austerlitz*. München: C. Hanser, 2001.

Spoerer, Mark. *500 Jahre Flachglas: 1487–1987*, Schorndorf: Hofmann, 1988.

NOTES

Weiden in der Oberpfalz

1. The mechanical drawing process, in which sheets of glass are drawn vertically out of molten glass, was invented in 1904 by Belgian Émile Fourcault and further advanced in 1916 by the American firm Libbey-Owens. The "float glass" process, invented in the 1950s by Briton Alastair Pilkington, involved floating the melted raw materials over a bath of molten metal. Flat glass has been produced almost exclusively by this method since the 1980s.

'The Lords Are Coming'

1. The photograph is undated, but judging from Erich's age it was taken around 1925. That would explain why my grandmother Berta, who died in 1923, isn't in the picture. My father may well have been the photographer.
2. At the height of the inflationary spiral, prices in Germany were rising so fast that waiters would climb on top of tables to call out new menu prices every half hour and workers literally brought wheelbarrows to work to collect their pay.

Confusion at the Cemetery

1. The vandals carted away the granite and marble pieces and sold them, according to a local historian. Some of the material was later used to pave the roads.
2. The SS, or *Schutzstaffel* [Protective Echelon], was founded by Hitler in 1925 as a small personal bodyguard unit and grew into a powerful paramilitary force.
3. *Vernichtung durch Arbeit* [Extermination through labor] was an SS slogan.
4. Peter Hohenhaus, "Flossenbürg Concentration Camp Memorial Site," accessed June 13, 2022, https://www.dark-tourism.com/index.php/15-countries/individual-chapters/218-flossenbuerg-concentration-camp.
5. Heinz Heger, *The Men with the Pink Triangle: The True Life-and-Death Story of Homosexuals in the Nazi Death Camps* (Alyson Books, rev. ed., 1994).
6. The American attack on Weiden began on April 21, 1945, with an artillery bombardment. The next day the Army moved in with tanks and occupied the city. A prison camp was set up where thousands of German soldiers were held until the war ended two weeks later.
7. The first such organization, the "Anti-Semitic People's Society of Weiden," was founded in 1893 by Heinrich Otto, the managing director of the Bauscher porcelain company in Weiden. It disbanded around 1908.

Starting Over

1. The *Bremen* was one of the swiftest and most luxurious ocean liners afloat. On her maiden voyage in 1929, she captured the coveted Blue Riband for the fastest Atlantic crossing, a distinction that had been held for nearly 20 years by Cunard's *Mauretania*. The *Bremen* made the crossing in 4 days, 14 hours, and 30 minutes at an average speed of 27.9 knots.
2. The SA, or *Sturmabteilung* [Assault Division], was the original paramilitary wing of the Nazi Party, and its violent tactics played a key role in Hitler's rise to power. The SA's primary purpose was to provide security at Nazi rallies and disrupt the meetings of opposing parties. Members became known as Brownshirts because of the color of their uniforms. The group was effectively disbanded in 1934 when dozens of SA leaders were executed during the so-called Night of the Long Knives.
3. The *Bremen*'s last transatlantic voyage began on the evening of August 30, 1939, two days before the outbreak of the war, when she steamed out of New York Harbor bound for Bremerhaven. Evading a British blockade, she crossed the Arctic Circle and dropped anchor in the Soviet port of Murmansk on September 6. She didn't make it back to her home port until December 13. During the war the *Bremen* served as a barracks ship for German troops. The Nazis intended to use her as a transport in Operation Sea Lion, the code name for their planned invasion of Great Britain, but on March 16, 1941, the ship was set on fire by a disgruntled cabin boy and gutted. Her remains were towed up the River Weser and destroyed by explosives, but parts of her hull are still visible today at low tide.
4. Although Underwood was based in New York, Dad's typewriter had a German keyboard.
5. "Refugees," Holocaust Encyclopedia, US Holocaust Memorial Museum, accessed June 13, 2022, https://encyclopedia.ushmm.org/content/en/article/refugees.
6. The Czech name is Karlovy Vary.
7. The average weekly salary in the United States in 1937 was $32.
8. Founded in 1868 and still in business today, J.R. Watkins was one of the largest direct-sales companies in the world at the time Dad joined it.
9. In January 1942, shortly after the US entered the war, the government-imposed restrictions on the movement of so-called enemy aliens – non-American citizens from Germany, Italy, and Japan.
10. The National Archives, which maintains military personnel records, has no record of Dad serving, but it's possible his information was lost in a 1973 fire that destroyed the files of millions of men and women who served in the military during the war. The Jewish Welfare Board, which compiled a comprehensive list of Jews who served in the US armed services during World War II, also has no record of my father.
11. *GI Jews*, a 2018 documentary about the more than half million Jewish Americans who fought in World War II, features several German-born Jews, including

Hollywood director Mel Brooks and Secretary of State Henry Kissinger.

Getting Out

1. The list of items also included one pair of pajamas [*Schlafrock*], 30 shirts, 36 pairs of socks, 18 linen collars, and two pairs of leggings.
2. An apparent reference to the Majdanek concentration camp outside Lublin, in German-occupied Poland.

Stormy Wedding

1. Daniel J. Sharfstein, "Saving the Race," *Legal Affairs* (March/April 2005). https://www.legalaffairs.org/issues/March-April-2005/feature_sharfstein_marapr05.msp.
2. The Spell case is the centerpiece of *Marshall*, a 2017 biopic about the future Supreme Court justice starring Chadwick Boseman.
3. William Brewster's father, Frederick Foster Brewster, was an industrialist who bequeathed his 25-acre Tudor-style estate to the city of New Haven to be used as a public park. The original owner of the property was Eli Whitney, the inventor of the cotton gin. With its rolling lawns studded by elms and oaks and enclosed by a high stone wall, Edgerton Park was one of my favorite refuges as a young man.
4. Bertha and her husband, Sam Roberts, owned a popular hot dog stand at an amusement park on the West Haven shore. Until it fell into disrepair and closed in the mid-1960s, Savin Rock was Connecticut's pale imitation of Coney Island. I have fond memories of going there with my family on balmy summer evenings to drive the bumper cars, ride the rickety rollercoaster, and chow down on grilled hot dogs and clams on the half shell.
5. Ukraine was then, and remains today, one of the world's largest grain exporters.
6. The most memorable event during my visit to Ukraine occurred not in Rzhyshchiv but in Kyiv, where I was arrested for taking photographs outside a military installation. I was hustled into a patrol car, driven to a police station and ordered to turn over my film. I rewound the film and opened my camera, but when the officers were looking the other way, I slipped the exposed roll into my pocket and handed them an unused one. Fortunately, they let me go before the switch was discovered. I must have been watching too many James Bond movies.
7. Mom was born in New Haven Hospital (now Yale New Haven Hospital), the same hospital where Richard and I – and George Bush the Younger – entered the world.
8. Mac, the first member of the family to graduate from college, went to Lafayette in eastern Pennsylvania – the same school Richard attended four decades later. He went on to graduate from Yale Law School and establish a successful career practicing family and marriage law in New Haven. He was active in local Democratic politics, winning election to a two-year term on the Board of Aldermen in 1940. He was also a terrific tennis player who captured the New

Haven Men's Singles Championship when he was only 16, a feat he repeated three years later. Nan attended a special program at Yale Music School that qualified her to teach music, but she never pursued a teaching career.

9. Two months later, in December 1946, an infamous meeting of Mafia dons organized by Lucky Luciano and Meyer Lansky at the Hotel Nacional in Havana laid the groundwork for transforming the Cuban capital into a seaside gambling resort.

Matriarchy

1. The medical term is iliofemoral thrombophlebitis.
2. Her boss, George Crawford, became the first Black corporation counsel for the city of New Haven.

Willow Street

1. The term stems from *schvartz*, Yiddish for black.

Big Gert and Little Bob

1. Yiddish for dressed up.
2. Sam Tower wrote a stamps column for the *New York Times*.

Different Dad

1. Yiddish for slaps on the ass.

Drugs, Deadheads, and Divine Light

1. In 2006, 30 years after Dad died and less than two years after Mom passed away, Richard lost a brief but painful battle with pancreatic cancer. He was 56.

Gay Boy

1. Yiddish for "Woe is me!"
2. Garland's popularity with queer men has been attributed to the fact that we identified with her struggles with substance abuse and men. As William Goldman put it in a 1969 *Esquire* article: "They are a persecuted group and they understand suffering. And so does Garland."
3. First published in 1969, *Everything You Always Wanted to Know About Sex* became a number 1 best-seller in 51 countries and inspired a Woody Allen film by the

same title.

Lost Portraits

1. He received two hours of Jewish religious education one afternoon a week, just as other students did in their religion. Unlike in the US, where religious instruction is prohibited in public schools, it is permitted in Germany.
2. Michael Brenner, *Am Beispiel Weiden: Jüdischer Alltag im Nationalsozialismus* [The Example of Weiden: Everyday Life for Jews Under National Socialism] (Würzburg: Arena, 1983). Michael went on to become a distinguished professor of Jewish history and the author of nine books. He holds teaching positions at Ludwig Maximilians University in Munich and American University in Washington and serves as international president of the Leo Baeck Institut, which is devoted to the study of the history and culture of German-speaking Jewry.

The Quest

1. The grandson of Otto's sister Rosa, Paul doesn't want his last name disclosed out of concern for his privacy.
2. Sebastian Schott, *Weiden a Mechtige Kehille: Eine Jüdische Gemeinde in der Oberpfalz vom Mittelalter bis zur Mitte des 20 Jahrhunderts* [Weiden a Strong Community: a Jewish Community in the Oberpfalz from the Middle Ages to the mid-20th century] (Pressath: Eckhard Bodner, 2003).
3. As a sovereign state within the German Empire, the Kingdom of Bavaria maintained its own army until 1919.
4. I learned about Otto's military service through Ancestry.com and the Bavarian State Archives.
5. University-bound students attended either an *Oberrealschule* or a gymnasium, which required two additional years of study.
6. The school's annual report lists Dad's *confession*, or religion, as *Isr*, for Israelite. The rest of the class consisted of 32 Catholics and 13 Protestants.

Glass Dynasty

1. Michael Müller, "Die Spieglas Dynastie 'Kupfer und Glaser' und die Glastütte Frankenreuth" [The Kupfer and Glaser Glass Dynasty and the Frankenreuth Glass Foundry], trans. P. Sinclair. *Rijo Research* (2012).
2. Samuel Kurinsky, *The Glassmakers: An Odyssey of the Jews* (Hippocrene Books, 1991).
3. The United States was for many years the largest market for Bavarian plate glass. In the 1880s, the US imported 87 percent of the value of Bavaria's entire plate-glass production.

4. New laws enacted in Austria-Hungary in 1867 and Germany in 1871 granted civil equality to Jews. Before then, Jews were restricted in which occupations they could practice and even where they could live.
5. Until the invention of "float glass" in the mid-20th century, grinding and polishing was an essential step in flat glass production because earlier methods produced glass sheets with rough surfaces and edges and poor transparency. It was especially important in mirror glass, which needed to be free of distortion and highly transparent. For centuries this work was done by hand, but machines were introduced around 1800 that made the process more efficient. Still, it often required a whole day to finish a single sheet of glass. For that reason, mirrors were still considered a luxury item well into the 20th century. Float glass, which involved floating melted raw materials at high temperature over a bath of molten metal, virtually eliminated the need for grinding and polishing. Flat glass has been produced almost exclusively by this method since the 1980s.
6. According to family lore, the couple actually spawned a baker's dozen, but I could find no evidence of a 13th child. A fire in the Waidhaus *Rathaus* destroyed some early records, so it's possible another child died in infancy and the birth and death certificates were lost.
7. Ignaz Glaser notebook from April 1, 1898 to April 31, 1899, as reported by Michael Müller.
8. Ibid.
9. Fürth was nicknamed the "Town of Mirrors" because of its concentration of mirror coating works. In the late 17th and 18th centuries, many artisans in newer trades like mirror manufacturing moved from the old imperial city of Nuremberg, where guilds dating to the Middle Ages created anti-competitive barriers, to the more liberal city of Fürth. The city was especially attractive to Jewish entrepreneurs who were not allowed to live in Nuremberg. Fürth had another, somewhat pejorative, sobriquet, "Franconian Jerusalem," because of its long history of welcoming Jews. When Emperor Leopold I expelled the entire Jewish population of Vienna in 1670 many upper-class Jews moved to Fürth. In 1807 nearly one out of five residents was Jewish, and by 1840 more than half of all Bavarian Jews lived in Fürth.
10. The casting and rolling process was invented in 1919 by German Max Bicheroux. The drawing process, in which glass sheets are drawn vertically out of the yellow-hot *metal*, or molten glass, was invented in 1904 by Belgian Émile Fourcault and further advanced in 1916 by the American firm Libbey-Owens. Mirror and flat glass were still being produced by these two methods until the 1960s, when the float glass process was developed.
11. Aloys died in 1905 at age 77 in Vienna, where he had been living since 1870.
12. Based on a letter from the city of Weiden to the Compensation Authority in Wiesbaden stemming from a claim my father made to recover assets and income my grandfather lost as a result of Nazi persecution.

A Brief History of Antisemitism in Germany

1. James F. Harris, *The People Speak! Anti-Semitism and Emancipation in 19th Century Bavaria* (University of Michigan Press, 1994).
2. Ibid., p. 252.

Gathering Storm

1. *Der Stürmer,* said to be Hitler's favorite newspaper, accused Jews of virtually every ill afflicting German society, from high unemployment and inflation to prostitution and the ritual murders of women and children. Hitler insisted the tabloid be displayed in special glass cases called *Stürmerkasten* to maximize public exposure. The publisher, Julius Streicher, also published several antisemitic books for children, including *Der Giftpilz* [The Poisonous Mushroom], which compared Jews to alluring but deadly mushrooms.
2. Half a century earlier, in August 1876, Weiden played host to another political bigwig when Karl Marx spent the night there on his way to Karlsbad. And a decade before that, in August 1867, philosopher Friedrich Nietzsche visited the city during a holiday trip to the Bohemian Forest.
3. Located on the grounds of an abandoned munitions factory, Dachau was the first Nazi concentration camp in Germany. It was opened on March 22, 1933, by Heinrich Himmler, then chief of the Munich police who went on to become the notorious commander of the SS and played a major role in the Holocaust. The camp was originally intended to hold political prisoners, but its purpose was later expanded to include Jews, homosexuals, forced laborers, and others. Dachau was notorious for its brutal treatment of prisoners and its design and organization became a model for other Nazi concentration camps. More than 32,000 people died there according to the records, but the actual death toll is believed to be much higher.
4. In June 1933 the Nazis banned the SPD throughout Germany, and the next month all political parties – except the NSDAP, of course – were made illegal.
5. Harbauer had derided Mayor Melchior Probst for his extravagant lifestyle, but after taking office the Nazi leader occupied his predecessor's private villa and gained a reputation of his own for lavish spending. "He lives like a real Nazi bigwig, far more luxurious and splendid than any of his predecessors," *Sopade,* an SPD publication, tutted.
6. Harbauer was removed from office on April 26, 1945, four days after the 11th US Tank Division rolled into Weiden, and he subsequently spent two years in an internment camp. In 1948 a "denazification" tribunal sentenced him to five years in a labor camp, but the sentence was commuted to house arrest because of ill health. He died in Weiden in 1966.

Daily Torment

1. According to Otto Marx, one of the organizers of the anti-Jewish boycotts in Weiden was the son of the managing director of the Bauscher porcelain company, which was located down the street from the Kupfer glass factory. Founded in Weiden in 1881, Bauscher was, and remains today, one of the city's largest employers. When its US agent, a Jewish man named Arthur Schiller, learned of the son's involvement in the boycott, he refused to represent the company any longer. In an effort to win him back, Bauscher invited Schiller to Weiden, but before he arrived company officials made sure to remove antisemitic slogans posted on the factory floor and warned employees to refrain from using the Nazi salute.
2. Marx wrote his account, a copy of which resides in the Weiden city archives, after he and his family fled to the United States in 1938.
3. In the early years of the Nazi regime, its primary targets were Social Democrats, communists, and other political foes. It's likely that Marx and other Jews sent to Dachau and other concentration camps during this period were targeted because of their political activities rather than their religion. It wasn't until after Kristallnacht, in November 1938, that Jews were sent to the camps in large numbers solely because of their religious identity.
4. Steinbrenner was one of the most infamous block leaders at Dachau, known for his demented laughter and capricious savagery. After the war he was sentenced to life in prison for the murder of two Jewish inmates. He was released from prison in 1962 and committed suicide two years later in a nursing home in Berchtesgaden, not far from Hitler's mountain retreat in the Bavarian Alps.
5. At least 85 people died during the purge, although the final death toll may have been in the hundreds, and more than a 1,000 perceived opponents were arrested. Most of the killings were carried out by the SS and the Gestapo, the secret police.
6. *Sarasota Herald Tribune* (via Associated Press), 1992.
7. Dubbed the "Jewel Box" because of its ornate baroque and rococo architecture, Dresden was decimated by American and British bombs near the end of the war. The controversial attack killed some 25,000 people, many of them civilians, and destroyed the city center.
8. Victor Klemperer, *I Will Bear Witness: A Diary of the Nazi Years, 1933-1941* (New York: Random House, 1998). The book became a huge best-seller in Germany when it was first published in 1995.
9. *Bayerische Ostmark,* or Bavarian Eastern March, was an administrative division of Nazi Germany comprised of the Oberpfalz, Lower Bavaria, and Upper Franconia.

Kristallnacht and Beyond

1. Earlier estimates put the death toll at 91, but historians now believe that hundreds of Jews were murdered or died in the immediate aftermath of the pogrom.
2. Sixteen Nazis and four police officers were killed in the failed coup d'état in Munich on November 8-9, 1923. Hitler was arrested and served nine months in prison, where he began to write his infamous political manifesto, *Mein Kampf* [My Struggle].
3. Johannes Laschinger, "Judenpogrome in Weiden und Amberg 1938" [Jewish Pogroms in Weiden and Amberg 1938] (Historical Club for Upper Palatinate and Regensburg, 2016). The study was based largely on files found in the public prosecutor's office in Weiden.
4. According to one survivor from the nearby city of Furth, some residents were less concerned about the violence committed against their Jewish neighbors than the unpleasantness of "seeing their pavements littered with glass splinters, torn overcoats, unhinged typewriters, beheaded teddy bears, and the Daliesque picture of half a piano laying across our busy main street." (Kristallnacht Memories of Edgar Rosenberg, Haiti Jewish Refugee Legacy Project).
5. It was in Wies' old house, which was occupied by a travel agency after the war, that I met one of his relatives during my first visit to Weiden in 1979.
6. Schott, *Weiden a Mechtige Kehille*.
7. Wies, it should be clear, was no angel either. In the same letter in which he accused the businessman of being friendly with Jews, Harbauer notes that Wies was "not a person who was opposed to Nazism" and that he had supported the party as far back as the Munich Beer Hall Putsch in 1923.
8. Schott, *Weiden a Mechtige Kehille*.
9. Hessen State Archives, Office for Control of Assets and Compensation, Dept. 519/3, No. 22313 (June 13, 1939).
10. Ibid., No. 22313 (August 10, 1939).
11. Ibid., No. 3885 (August 16, 1939).
12. Ibid., No. 22313 (June 30, 1939).
13. The school was a successor of the Hoch Conservatory, founded in 1878, which had a worldwide reputation in the late-19th and early-20th centuries. When the Nazis came to power in 1933, 13 members of the teaching staff who were Jewish or foreign were removed from their positions. Although I didn't notice them when I was there because it was dark, I later learned that *Stolpersteine* had been laid in the sidewalk outside the building in memory of two residents who, like my grandfather, had perished in Theresienstadt.

Otto's Choice

1. The plight of Jews trying to flee Nazi Germany was illustrated by the ill-fated voyage of the SS *St. Louis*. The German luxury liner set sail from Hamburg to Havana on May 13, 1939, with 937 passengers, most of them Jewish refugees.

After the Cuban and US governments refused to allow the ship to dock it was forced to return to Europe, where more than 250 of the passengers died in the Holocaust.

2. Otto was 19 when his family moved from Frankenreuth, on the Czech border, to Weiden. With the exception of a four-year period between 1927 and 1931, when he lived in Schlangenbad, a spa town outside Wiesbaden, and the four months he was held captive in Theresienstadt, he lived in Weiden his entire adult life.

A Retirement Home in Bohemia

1. These numbers appear on a post-war compilation and might not be the original numbers used by the Nazis.
2. Otto's brother Moritz, who was married to a Christian woman, was an unfortunate exception to this policy. He was deported to Mauthausen in Austria on September 19, 1942, and died five days later.
3. Yad Vashem. http://db.yadvashem.org/deportation/transportDetails.html?language=en&itemId=5092427.
4. Ibid.
5. Ibid.
6. The SS or *Schutzstaffel* was the Nazi paramilitary group charged with security, surveillance, and terror. The units responsible for running concentration camps were known as *SS-Totenkopfverbände* or Death Head units.
7. Ernst's wife, Teddy, gave birth to their first child, Monique in November 1941. A second daughter, Odette, was born in June 1945.
8. W.G. Sebald, *Austerlitz* (München: C. Hanser, 2001).
9. Redlich, who was in charge of the youth welfare department at the ghetto, was deported to Auschwitz with his wife and son in 1944. Before his deportation he concealed his diary in an attic, where it was discovered by Czech workers in 1967.
10. Yad Vashem.
11. Esther Levy, *Legacies, Lies and Lullabies: The World of a Second Generation Holocaust Survivor* (First Edition Design Publishing, 2013).
12. Based on a report by Rabbi Leopold Neuhaus, a Jewish spiritual leader from Frankfurt am Main, on July 21, 1944.
13. Joseph, the brother of Marie Antoinette, named the military stronghold after their mother, Empress Maria Theresa.
14. "Arthur Karl Heinz Oertelt," Holocaust Encyclopedia, US Holocaust Memorial Museum, accessed June 13, 2022, https://encyclopedia.ushmm.org/content/en/id-card/arthur-karl-heinz-oertelt.
15. The National Archives (UK), accessed June 13, 2022, https://www.nationalarchives.gov.uk/education/resources/holocaust/theresienstadt/.
16. US Holocaust Memorial Museum.
17. The former was a big concession by the Nazis, who regarded jazz or swing as "degenerate" and banned it in Germany because two of its leading practitioners, Benny Goodman and Artie Shaw, were Jewish.
18. The film is sometimes mistakenly called *Der Führer schenkt den Juden eine Stadt* [The Leader Gives the Jews a Town as a Gift].

19. Most of the film was destroyed, but some footage has survived and is available at the Terezín Museum and the Imperial War Museum in London.

Dad's Silence

1. Karen Berman, "The Children of the Survivors," *New York Times*, October 27, 1996. Tragically, Karen died in October 2019 of pancreatic cancer, the same disease that took my brother 13 years earlier.

On the Fence

1. Not his real name.
2. I recently tracked down Lenny in Massachusetts, where he has been a public school teacher for decades, and we met for the first time in nearly half a century at a restaurant outside Boston.

Getting Closer

1. I was three credits shy of earning my Bachelor's. I took a class at Southern Connecticut State College in New Haven that summer to close the deal.

Final Days

1. Reputed to be the oldest watering hole in New York, Pete's has appeared in numerous films and television programs, including *Seinfeld, Ragtime, Law & Order, and Sex and the City*. Legend has it that O. Henry, who lived down the street, penned his acclaimed short story "The Gift of the Magi" at the tavern in 1905.
2. The writer Charlotte Devree likened Gramercy Park to "a Victorian gentleman who has refused to die." ("Private Life of a Park," *New York Times,* Dec. 8, 1957.)
3. Irving Berlin and Leonard Bernstein were among the many celebrities who frequented Lüchow's before it closed in the early-80s.

Guest of the City

1. It states that 34 Jews from Weiden were murdered in the Holocaust, but the actual number is 56. That error was corrected in a memorial plaque unveiled in 2020 in the new City Hall, which lists the names of all 56 Jewish victims, my grandfather Otto and his sister Mina among them, as well as 32 others.

Eduard and Fanni Return

1. Erich and Ruth had met in Germany before the war. While Erich followed my father's footsteps and immigrated to the US, Ruth went to England. They were married in 1946 via a transcontinental phone call between London and Topeka, Kansas, one of the few states where marriage by telephone was legal.
2. Schott, *Weiden a Mechtige Kehille*.
3. Inge's father served in the German army and was taken prisoner in France, where he was held in a POW camp for several years before returning home in 1948.

Back to Weiden

1. Given Weiden's proximity to the Czech border, it was one of the first cities in the American occupation zone that displaced people from eastern Europe and the Baltic States passed through as they headed west. Several camps were established in Weiden to accommodate the refugees, many of whom were Jews liberated from concentration camps or fleeing antisemitism in Poland. At the end of 1946, almost 700 Jews were living in the city, according to Dr. Schott, though most of them eventually moved on to Palestine and other places.

Article 116

1. Our German naturalization papers finally came through in August 2021, followed by our passports a few months later.

AMSTERDAM PUBLISHERS HOLOCAUST LIBRARY

The series **Holocaust Survivor Memoirs World War II** consists of the following autobiographies of survivors:

Outcry. Holocaust Memoirs, by Manny Steinberg

Hank Brodt Holocaust Memoirs. A Candle and a Promise, by Deborah Donnelly

The Dead Years. Holocaust Memoirs, by Joseph Schupack

Rescued from the Ashes. The Diary of Leokadia Schmidt, Survivor of the Warsaw Ghetto, by Leokadia Schmidt

My Lvov. Holocaust Memoir of a twelve-year-old Girl, by Janina Hescheles

Remembering Ravensbrück. From Holocaust to Healing, by Natalie Hess

Wolf. A Story of Hate, by Zeev Scheinwald with Ella Scheinwald

Save my Children. An Astonishing Tale of Survival and its Unlikely Hero, by Leon Kleiner with Edwin Stepp

Holocaust Memoirs of a Bergen-Belsen Survivor & Classmate of Anne Frank, by Nanette Blitz Konig

Defiant German - Defiant Jew. A Holocaust Memoir from inside the Third Reich, by Walter Leopold with Les Leopold

In a Land of Forest and Darkness. The Holocaust Story of two Jewish Partisans, by Sara Lustigman Omelinski

Holocaust Memories. Annihilation and Survival in Slovakia, by Paul Davidovits

From Auschwitz with Love. The Inspiring Memoir of Two Sisters' Survival, Devotion and Triumph Told by Manci Grunberger Beran & Ruth Grunberger Mermelstein, by Daniel Seymour

Remetz. Resistance Fighter and Survivor of the Warsaw Ghetto, by Jan Yohay Remetz

My March Through Hell. A Young Girl's Terrifying Journey to Survival, by Halina Kleiner with Edwin Stepp

---

The series **Holocaust Survivor True Stories WWII** consists of the following biographies:

Among the Reeds. The true story of how a family survived the Holocaust, by Tammy Bottner

A Holocaust Memoir of Love & Resilience. Mama's Survival from Lithuania to America, by Ettie Zilber

Living among the Dead. My Grandmother's Holocaust Survival Story of Love and Strength, by Adena Bernstein Astrowsky

Heart Songs. A Holocaust Memoir, by Barbara Gilford

Shoes of the Shoah. The Tomorrow of Yesterday, by Dorothy Pierce

Hidden in Berlin. A Holocaust Memoir, by Evelyn Joseph Grossman

Separated Together. The Incredible True WWII Story of Soulmates Stranded an Ocean Apart, by Kenneth P. Price, Ph.D.

The Man Across the River. The incredible story of one man's will to survive the Holocaust, by Zvi Wiesenfeld

If Anyone Calls, Tell Them I Died. A Memoir, by Emanuel (Manu) Rosen

The House on Thrömerstrasse. A Story of Rebirth and Renewal in the Wake of the Holocaust, by Ron Vincent

Dancing with my Father. His hidden past. Her quest for truth. How Nazi Vienna shaped a family's identity, by Jo Sorochinsky

The Story Keeper. Weaving the Threads of Time and Memory - A Memoir, by Fred Feldman

Krisia's Silence. The Girl who was not on Schindler's List, by Ronny Hein

Defying Death on the Danube. A Holocaust Survival Story, by Debbie J. Callahan with Henry Stern

A Doorway to Heroism. A decorated German-Jewish Soldier who became an American Hero, by Rabbi W. Jack Romberg

The Shoemaker's Son. The Life of a Holocaust Resister, by Laura Beth Bakst

The Redhead of Auschwitz. A True Story, by Nechama Birnbaum

Land of Many Bridges. My Father's Story, by Bela Ruth Samuel Tenenholtz

Creating Beauty from the Abyss. The Amazing Story of Sam Herciger, Auschwitz Survivor and Artist, by Lesley Ann Richardson

On Sunny Days We Sang. A Holocaust Story of Survival and Resilience, by Jeannette Grunhaus de Gelman

Painful Joy. A Holocaust Family Memoir, by Max J. Friedman

I Give You My Heart. A True Story of Courage and Survival, by Wendy Holden

In the Time of Madmen, by Mark A. Prelas

Monsters and Miracles. Horror, Heroes and the Holocaust, by Ira Wesley Kitmacher

Flower of Vlora. Growing up Jewish in Communist Albania, by Anna Kohen

Aftermath: Coming of Age on Three Continents. A Memoir, by Annette Libeskind Berkovits

Not a real Enemy. The True Story of a Hungarian Jewish Man's Fight for Freedom, by Robert Wolf

The Glassmaker's Son. Looking for the World my Father left behind in Nazi Germany, by Peter Kupfer

Zaidy's War, by Martin Bodek

The Apprentice of Buchenwald. The True Story of the Teenage Boy Who Sabotaged Hitler's War Machine, by Oren Schneider

---

The series **Jewish Children in the Holocaust** consists of the following autobiographies of Jewish children hidden during WWII in the Netherlands:

Searching for Home. The Impact of WWII on a Hidden Child, by Joseph Gosler

See You Tonight and Promise to be a Good Boy! War memories, by Salo Muller

Sounds from Silence. Reflections of a Child Holocaust Survivor, Psychiatrist and Teacher, by Robert Krell

Sabine's Odyssey. A Hidden Child and her Dutch Rescuers, by Agnes Schipper

The Journey of a Hidden Child, by Harry Pila with Robin Black

---

The series **New Jewish Fiction** consists of the following novels, written by Jewish authors. All novels are set in the time during or after the Holocaust.

The Corset Maker. A Novel, by Annette Libeskind Berkovits

Escaping the Whale. The Holocaust is over. But is it ever over for the next generation? by Ruth Rotkowitz

When the Music Stopped. Willy Rosen's Holocaust, by Casey Hayes

Hands of Gold. One Man's Quest to Find the Silver Lining in Misfortune, by Roni Robbins

The Girl Who Counted Numbers. A Novel, by Roslyn Bernstein

There was a garden in Nuremberg. A Novel, by Navina Michal Clemerson

The Butterfly and the Axe, by Omer Bartov

Good For a Single Journey, by Helen Joyce

The series **Holocaust Books for Young Adults** consists of the following novels, based on true stories:

The Boy behind the Door. How Salomon Kool Escaped the Nazis. Inspired by a True Story, by David Tabatsky

Running for Shelter. A True Story, by Suzette Sheft

The Precious Few. An Inspirational Saga of Courage based on True Stories, by David Twain with Art Twain

Want to be an AP book reviewer?

Reviews are very important in a world dominated by the social media and social proof. Please drop us a line if you want to join the *AP review team*. We will then add you to our list of advance reviewers. No strings attached, and we promise that we will not be spamming you.

info@amsterdampublishers.com

www.ingramcontent.com/pod-product-compliance
Lightning Source LLC
LaVergne TN
LVHW091547070526
838199LV00024B/574/J